I'VE NEVER MADE A MISTAKE...
ONCE I THOUGHT I DID, BUT I WAS WRONG

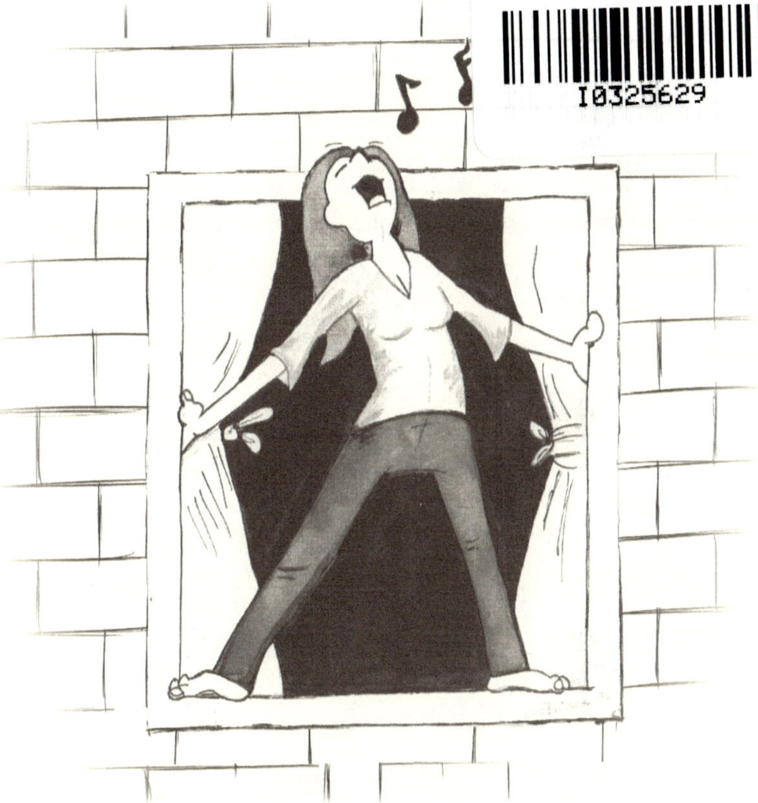

*A book with an edge
to keep you off the ledge*

JOAN ARENT

DENVER, CO

Text and illustrations copyright © 2019 by Joan Arent. All rights reserved.

No part of this publication may be reproduced or transmitted in any form or by any means, electronic or mechanical, including photocopying, recording, or by any information storage and retrieval system, now known or to be invented, without permission in writing from the publisher.

For information regarding permissions, contact the publisher at:

Joan Arent, It Stiks Publishing
8200 E. Pacific Place, Unit 203, Denver, CO 80231
JoanofArt@joanarent.com

The stories in this book are based upon true events and characters. However, some names, locales, and descriptive details have been modified to protect the privacy of individuals whose lives have intersected with Joan Arent.

Author: Joan Arent
Illustrator: Joan Arent
Editor: Jennifer Thomas, Beyond Words Editing
Designer: Jennifer Thomas, Beyond Words Editing
Project Coordinator: Jessica Ricalde
Artwork Consultant: Rob Aukerman
Front Cover Art: Joan Arent
Front Cover Design: Rob Aukerman

LCCN: 2018911425
ISBN: 978-0-9885979-4-5 (Softcover)
ISBN: 978-0-9885979-5-2 (eBook)

BISAC Subject Headings:
    SEL016000   SELF-HELP / Personal Growth / Happiness
    SEL024000   SELF-HELP / Self-Management / Stress Management
    HUM000000 HUMOR / General

First Edition 2019
Published in the United States of America

DEDICATION

**To my reasons for living:
My husband, my son, and my daughter**

Thank you for encouraging me to write, illustrate, and paint—especially when the alternatives were doing dishes, carpooling, picking up dog poop, or calling your teacher to explain why you were putting bras and underwear on street signs.

I appreciate all your patience, love, and support.

To Mom and Dad

Thanks for giving me good excuses for all my blunders.

Introducing me to the idea "I've never made a mistake…once I thought I did but I was wrong" helped me to believe and understand that each "mistake" was in fact a learning opportunity.

To my siblings and your families

The laughter we share helps mold me.

CONTENTS

Preface   1
Life: A Leap of Faith

Introduction   7
Lessons From the Grim Reaper

1 Fifty Shades of Grey   17
Whip Your Life Into Shape

2 Why I Eat My Young   23
Lessons Come in All Flavors

3 Roll With It   29
Sucking It Up to Survive

4 Joanie in a Lamp   35
Shifting Your Poo-spective

5 Don't Sleep With Fabio   41
Put Your Stress to Rest

6 A Tale of Three Pool Boys   47
Just Keep Swimming

I'VE NEVER MADE A MISTAKE...

7 **A Bitch, A Bitch** 51
Life's a Bitch—Enjoy It

8 **Eliza, Eliza** 59
Gone But Not Forgotten: Lessons in the Unseen

9 **Cabbage Patch Kiddie Breasts** 65
Find Your Buddies

10 **Joan O Fart** 71
Stik-y Business

11 **Whiny-the-Poo** 79
And Triggers Too

12 **Crimes Against My Sanity** 85
The Answers Are in How You Play Your Cards

13 **My Country—Right or Wrong?** 91
A Lottery With No Winners

14 **Do You Have GAS?** 97
Set Your Boundaries

15 **The Art of MANEtainance** 103
The Affordable Hair Act in Action

16 **A Forty-Year-Old Virgin** 109
STDs Without the Fun

Contents

17 LSD, Sit-Ins, and Me   119
You Can Redirect Your Life

18 The Tormentor   125
Alzheimer's Sucks

19 Wait, Wait—Don't Shoot!   143
Grief Can Be a Loaded Gun

20 Music Gave Speech to My Angel   153
A Dance-Date With Destiny

21 Laugh of the Day   167
Putting the Man Back in Your Mango

22 Walt Disney's Cough   173
Expel Your Creative Juices to Take Care of You

23 The Sound of Mucus   179
How to Escape the Phlegm in Your Life

24 Parachuting With a Purpose   187
"If at first you don't succeed... skydiving may not be for you!"

25 Save a Horse, Ride a Cowboy   195
Your Attitude Determines Your Ride

26	**Twitch, Twitch—I Can't Stop This Twitch** *Can't They Let Sleeping Dogs Lie?*	203
27	**Last Dance** *Lisa Jean: The Perfect Storm*	215
28	**I've Never Made a Mistake…** *Once I Thought I Did, But I Was Wrong—DEAD Wrong*	227
	Eliza, Eliza	234
	Acknowledgments	236
	About the Author	239
	Lisa Jean's Rock Star Memorial Fund	240

I'VE NEVER MADE A MISTAKE...
ONCE I THOUGHT I DID, BUT I WAS WRONG

PREFACE

Life: A Leap of Faith

P*rince Charming, not yet transformed from a frog, leaps toward me for love's fifth kiss. Puckered up...springing for joy at the prospect of everlasting happiness...heart afire...rejoicing in each breath...embracing life and all its dreams, promises, hopes...imagining a bright future.*

Brilliant rays of light create an effervescent glow on the figure vaulting my way. *SPLAT...thump, thump!* All is lost...I've smacked him with my car, not my lips.

Life is a leap of faith, similar to that of my amphibian prince who was just hopping along seeking more from his existence. Our journey is unknown, filled with twists and turns. My Prince Charming's dreams were changed in the blink of an eye, sideswiped by a sparkly blue MINI Coop.

A sudden blast of death can alter the course of your life with endless ripples of loss. Imagine Sleeping Beauty forever sawing Z's because Prince Charming is ten feet under—or, in this case, roadkill.

Then again, think of Cinderella asserting her power, deciding one can't wait around forever. Picture Snow White rejoicing in her transformation from codependence to independence—and, in losing her Prince Charming, discovering she's a lesbian.

In the movie *Shrek,* Fiona's presumed "Prince Charming," Lord Farquaad, would have left her sad, miserable, and—if she was lucky—

divorced, had she married him. Her Happily Ever After came in finding the perfect ogre to suit her green personality.

Happily Ever After is how you define the life you want—how you live, breathe, and imagine it.

In my youth, I had hopes, dreams, and a well-planned future. I believed that if I tried hard enough and dreamed the impossible, my pumpkin would turn into a golden carriage.

But death is the Wicked Witch. The ultimate triumph over evil, I discovered, is sustaining life.

A death sentence can hit with the force of a locomotive: unexpected, traumatic, and instantaneous. Less shocking but just as painful, it can be like taking a bite of a poison apple, its bitter gases seeping through you, slowly robbing you of breath as it envelopes you in its cold-blooded, remorseless grip, sucking away your power and sense of self.

As the princess in this fairy tale, I have been closely affected by both kinds of death: a swallow of toxic fruit and the slam of a vehicular transport. Each time, I rewrote my own fairy tale and, unlike my hapless amphibian, bounded onwards towards my happy ending.

Life, I've learned, is a series of slumps, bumps, and triumphs. We each have hardships that manifest in different shapes and sizes. Yet, each hardship ignites growth and achievement in unexpected ways.

I have written this book because my life and my perception of life are both twisted. What was your first clue: my blue MINI sporting Kermit as a hood ornament, or Snow White the Dyke?

I am inspired by the work of Erma Bombeck, Far Side Cartoons by Gary Larson (what better go-to for a completely fresh viewpoint of the world?), *All I Really Need to Know I Learned in Kindergarten*

Preface

by Robert Fulghum, *Rejection Proof* by Jia Jiang, and *Don't Sweat the Small Stuff* by Richard Carlson. Each writer has influenced how I've approached life and the writing of this book.

My warped sense of humor is what helps me laugh through the hard times. It inspires me to keep writing, creating, and doing the Himalayan shuffle—to put one step in front of the other and B-R-E-A-T-H-E.

How to Use This Book

This book is like the Internet. It is meant to provide at-your-fingertips information, entertainment, problem-solving solutions, laughs, and your own mind games to win.

Each chapter has an antagonist and a protagonist. The antagonist is the villain in your life, your own personal Darth Vader. He is the evildoer that slinks and slams his way through your reality, blinding you with his light saber rather than providing light at the end of the tunnel. His diabolical ways are like a hot breath on a ventilator, creating dark and menacing types of stress in different forms: nights of tormented sleep, difficult people, aging, family circuses, unthinkable losses, Dilbert-ian dilemmas, life-sucking relationships, and hallway sex (you know—when you and your significant other are so mad at each other, the only intimacy you share is exchanging "f--- you's" as you pass each other in the hall).

The protagonist is the good gal. Like Princess Leia, you can learn from her coping skills: how to pack an Uzi loaded with a sense of humor while being besieged by a work curmudgeon who has the intelligence of an ant in heat; how to resist torture from the kids' "new math" homework when your brain is too old to know math at all; how to believe in a good outcome even when it's hard just to get past the dirty laundry; how to help others without giving up on yourself; how to radiate beauty even when under fire from baby spit or grey hairs.

Each day of your life has an avalanche of antagonists, but with a twisted take and an attitude of amusement, it can overflow with protagonists. Like Darth Vader and Princess Leia, some bits of my stories have been invented for the sake of adventure, yet the honesty of character is still present.

The lines between good and evil can be blurred, but with the help of this book you will:

- Play and learn from characters like Magic Mike, the Genie in a Lamp, Fabio, a trio of Pool Boys, and a drag queen—congregating and collaborating to forge new perspectives that will help you with the rest of this list.
- Trek through the treacherous waters of life, which flow in the form of emotions, confusion, and hardships.
- Paddle your way to happiness and success by embracing the funny in the not-so-funny.
- Unearth jewels of wisdom and treasures of strategies that build resistance to your challenges.
- Triumph in the game called life.

Like life, this book includes sad, happy, dark, sexy, silly, and edgy humor. I believe I am as unique as they come, but so are you, and we all share similar worries, aches, pains, dilemmas, and challenges.

Preface

Just like the Web, surf these stories for the wave that will carry you through the day. Tap into them like the Weather app: when thunder and lightning are rumbling and warning signs are flashing—stop, read a chapter, and withstand any gale. Even when skies are clear and you're bathing in the warm sunshine of life, use the book to gather an understanding of what's ahead and prepare for how you're going to get through that day. Are you going to whip out your galoshes to maneuver through the poop puddles, or are you going to use sunscreen and an imaginary bubble to protect you from the harshness of the world?

Your greatest hero is your perception. It can provide you with Superman-sized navigational powers. You may not be Aladdin, Elsa, or Princess Leia, but by equipping yourself with humor, you can make your life a box-office hit.

You'll get to sit on Joan's Throne! You will look in that mirror and tell the Evil Queen: "Yo, She-Devil! Just because you have issues, I am not going into hiding with a bunch of men who never reached puberty. I am the fairest of them all—with or without a kiss from some guy in tights and a cape."

You will reign!!!

INTRODUCTION

Lessons From the Grim Reaper

"I've never made a mistake…once I thought I did, but I was wrong." This contorted catchphrase uttered by Charles Schulz's spitfire heroine, Lucy Van Pelt, was printed on my dad's coffee mug as I was growing up. It was one of my dad's many beloved sayings that made me think…and think again.

The phrase is like a Rubik's Cube: entertaining, perplexing, colorful, and shifty. Its words unraveled in my mind like a ball of yarn tossed around by a kitten. I chased them as a child, much like trying to catch a butterfly. *Hmmm… I pondered. Is it bad to make mistakes?*

I often chastised myself for not being perfect. Growing up with four brothers and three sisters was kind of like living with the seven dwarfs—except my siblings were Cranky, Cutie, Sloppy, Giggles, Sneaky, Bouncy, and Shorty in a three-bedroom dwelling with a mother who worked nights and slept days, and a dad who did the opposite. A lot of tough love was passed around.

But I embraced my dad's words, applauding the thought that life is easier if we believe we never make mistakes; rather, we learn lessons. Dad made the heavies of each day lighter by putting a humorous spin on what felt like a big deal. You couldn't get bogged down when his voice was in your head saying: *Don't take yourself so seriously.* A thing that seemed so important lost its steam once he shared his funny perspective on the matter.

Dad's interpretations were shaped by poverty, the deaths of his father and a sibling when he was young, and his own will to survive. He held his coffee mug like a badge of honor, reminding us every day that he'd never made a mistake…once he thought he did, but he was wrong. I am now the proud owner of that mug and all it stands for.

My parents taught me to laugh at my imperfections rather than beat myself up for being human. I now strive to tackle life with a sense of jocularity and optimism, to behold the mug of life as half full rather than half empty. It's not always an easy road, but I like to travel with a suitcase full of what I've dubbed "perception with a positive twist."

Life Is Hard, Death Is Harder

The Grim Reaper has repeatedly thrown his scythe in my path: six very important people in my life have died. And their passing has shaped my reality.

Introduction

Before all these losses, I was resigned to the day-to-day grind. I found my existence hard and full of hassles. And I thought how I was living was as good as it got.

Death has a way of shifting your focus. It helps you measure your waking hours more accurately, similar to having the Ghosts of Christmas Past, Present, and Future come for dinner and refuse to leave. What better way to psychoanalyze yourself than to philosophize as you watch Mickey Mouse, Donald Duck, Dopey, and Goofy play out *Mickey's Christmas Carol*, assessing how you have lived and how you want to live?

Throughout my life, health crises have threatened my well-being. In fifth grade, a bruise morphed into a tumor, terrifying my parents—but for me, five days in the hospital was an adventure. A doctor once told me I might have ovarian cancer; I told her I didn't have time for cancer. Many more scares came…I adjusted. From ages ten to thirty-six, I endured cancer diagnoses on my shin, cervix, ovary, and breast; a cyst burst; violent food allergies; four surgeries; and a ten-year standing date with five different physical therapists. We didn't catch dinner and a movie.

I lost my brother Matt in the Vietnam War. He was twenty-one and I was in sixth grade. He'd been my knight in shining armor who rescued me as I braved wild animals, intense heat, and strangers in a foreign land when I ran away at five years old. I made it to the end of the block feeling like I had crossed the Serengeti. He coaxed me back home with a bag of pretzels. Never let anyone tell you I'm easy.

When Matt was drafted, he and my oldest brother were put in the war zone of Vietnam at the same time. That wasn't supposed to be.

I'VE NEVER MADE A MISTAKE...

I remember coming home from school for lunch and answering the door to a man dressed in a green uniform. I smiled; he didn't. As I dished up my soup in the kitchen, I overheard him tell my dad that his second oldest son had stepped on a landmine. My dad woke my mom, who was sleeping after her night shift as a nurse. As he was busy breaking my mother's heart, I juggled my own emotions alone in the basement. Eventually they came and shared the news with me.

A few days later, I went back to school thinking I was strong enough to handle Matt's loss. I walked into my classroom and burst into tears.

My nephew died from leukemia at only six years old. He was diagnosed at age one and a half. I was in my twenties. He was a beautiful child and a fighter with the strength to adapt to hardships no one should have to endure, ever. He knew death was a force in his life, but at age four, how much can one really understand? When he traveled to Washington state for a bone marrow transplant, my young niece—having heard he was going to "Seattle"—asked, "Who is Attle?"

He saw Attle; she didn't help.

My dad lost his battle to strokes and a heart attack at age sixty-seven. I was twenty-eight. He never got to be a grandpa to my children, and they know him only through the sense of humor he passed down, alive through me and my memories.

Through all of this, I had no idea that these losses were just a prelude to the worst to come. Death would move into my heart and make itself a home.

On April 16, 1994, I took a home pregnancy test. It came back positive. I wrote a note to my husband, Allen, that said: *Hi, I am your soon-to-be baby daughter.* (That last part was a guess!) I taped it to the test, wrapped the whole thing up, and presented it to him and our two-year-old son, Bob, at dinner.

Introduction

I paused on the poignancy of the date. It was the date my brother Matt had died years before.

In the subsequent months, we prepared with great anticipation and joy for our second child. I had correctly prognosticated we were having a girl, and we called her "Bumpette." This was in homage to my first pregnancy, when we'd called our son "Bumper" because a friend said my stomach walked into the room before I did. We decorated the nursery, prepared Bob to expect the unexpected, and hurried to get work done that would be a challenge to complete with two small children.

At my five-month prenatal exam, the doctor said to me: "The baby seems a little small. Do you want to have an ultrasound?"

"I don't know—do I?" I replied.

"No, don't worry," came the answer. "Everything will be fine."

I often reflect on if we had done that ultrasound. Would that have prepared me for the oncoming train soon to run us over with heartbreak?

On December 15, 1994, I went into false labor. Uncle Don and Aunt Edna came to be with Bob so that we could go to the hospital. Twenty-four hours came and went with Bumpette in no hurry to say hello to her family. So back home I went.

Three days later, I went to the doctor for a checkup. "She isn't moving much," I told him. The doctor told me to schedule an ultrasound. The receptionist scoured her appointment book, but she couldn't find an opening for another five days.

"That seems kind of far away," I said.

"Oh, don't worry," she assured me. "Everything will be fine."

The night before my ultrasound, I dreamed Bumpette had died. The nightmare was so real, I brought Bob in to lie with me.

Two days before Christmas at 11:05 a.m., I went to see my OB/GYN. I laid on the exam table as the ultrasound tech searched and searched my belly for a heartbeat. Complete silence. She paused and asked the doctor to come in. But I still didn't suspect Bumpette was dead.

When the doctor broke the news, I let shock envelope me in denial, a cushion to the pain. Everything was not fine.

I remember calling Allen to tell him our daughter was gone before she was here.

But she still needed to come.

I was in labor for hours and delivered her that evening. On December 23rd, our daughter Eliza died from complications of a disease I could have picked up from touching a grocery cart. It's called cytomegalovirus (CMV) and she most likely contracted it when I was around one month pregnant. She never had a chance.

Many have asked if delivering her was hard. For me, it was the last thing I could do for her. It was the doorway to something better. One knows not what "better" is, but I have to believe there was a reason for my carrying her to full-term and then losing her. Perhaps I offered her a connection to another place and time, or another life. I don't know, so all I can do is hope: hope that her time in my life was as important to her as it was to me.

The Winds of Change

When Eliza died, a tornado of grief picked me up like a lawn chair and dropped me in a foreign desert. Nothing would ever be the same. The impact was such, that I would have to change my entire way of living if I were to survive in the devastating heat. If this was as good as it got, I had some work to do.

Before Eliza died, I'd felt sorry for myself—like I was unlucky. I got annoyed because the bank clerk wasn't moving fast enough, and angry when I was put on hold on the phone for too long. Life was one big challenge. I believed that I had bad *days,* not just bad moments or situations. *I* always got in the most time-consuming lines at the grocery store; *I* was not meant to get that last parking spot.

I tried to live with a sense of fun and spontaneity, but my mood was derailed by downer reactions to things. I was a little green creature with a target on my head, leaping into puddles too deep and reeds too high and getting my tongue stuck to tree trunks while trying to zap dinner.

After Eliza died, I shifted my way of thinking—it was the only way to survive. I decided to let go of the small things that I couldn't control in order to make room for what was important. How very little it mattered that I didn't get that last spot in the parking lot.

And the ride only got bumpier. I struggled with being a mom who was adrift. I had baby clothes and a nursery, but no baby. Standing in a checkout line, no longer caring about the length of it and repulsed by the food, my body betrayed me yet again: I started leaking milk when a baby cried two aisles over. Here I was, in agony so unbearable I had no appetite, yet my body was prepared to nurture a baby—any baby—as my burdened breasts declared.

And through all of this, I still had my son who needed me. But how could I take care of him when I could barely take care of myself? I was Rapunzel—a princess without a purpose, tangled in my emotions. I just wanted freedom from my pain.

I had to choose not to die with Eliza. I needed to grab positive thinking by the reins and hold on, because who knew when and how my life might change again in a major way. Like that frog leaping into the light, reality can be shattered.

If it weren't for my son and the support of my husband, my reality might have been different. Bob gave me purpose. When he saw me crying, he would come over and wipe my tears. Then he would go back to playing with his brightly colored blocks. He was so comforting. I would give into my exhaustion and fall asleep while rocking him. He found that quite entertaining.

Allen suffered through his own pain while taking on the to-do list. He got things done while I recovered. Going into action was his therapy.

How did I not die with my child? Eliza's loss gave me the tenacity to dream of another pregnancy, another child in my arms, a chance to win at what I'd lost.

After Eliza died, I miscarried nine times. The first seven children I named; after that, I ran out of stamina and names. Our family portrait included only my husband, my son, and myself. The black silhouettes surrounding us were the shadows of Eliza and the nine other children not meant to be. My body was my battlefield. My mind had to be my fortress.

But my body made it clear that it was not designed for pregnancies. After losing Eliza, I lived with chronic pain for nine years, at times so bad that I couldn't sleep, sit, or stand without major torment. And the doctors couldn't figure out what was wrong. I was without a compass. My well-planned future was writing its own endings and they were all the wrong kinds.

But I didn't give up. I held on to the humor I had learned from my family as I fought my way down briar-brindled paths that were dark and harsh.

And I still believed in the impossible. But after nine miscarriages I felt defeated. I was told I had a translocated gene, which gave me a fifty-percent chance of having another child. The math never did equate.

After six years of genetic and fertility doctors, pills, shots, and in-vitro fertilization, Allen and I decided to adopt. Reaching this decision had been heart-wrenching, because agency after agency shared not only success stories but also the devastating reality of adopting children with fetal alcohol syndrome, waits of up to ten years, and birth moms changing their minds. I didn't know if I had it in me to endure another loss—or even the unknown. But in the end, I felt it was most important to fulfill my longing for another child. We signed up with an agency on February 1st.

On March 19th, Anna, the daughter of my dreams, was born. I was at her birth. I was one of the lucky ones.

The fight was worth it because I now have a beautiful family of five, including Eliza. My daughter and son bring me great joy and laughter 'til I pee my pants. My family is my anchor in the rough seas.

Eventually I grew stronger and more resilient. I learned compassion I could only have learned through the hard knocks of life. I embraced the joy of the big accomplishments and let go of the minor disappointments.

The Joy of Joanisms

Over the years, friends have dubbed certain things I've said "Joanisms." They've quoted back to me quips or thoughts—many of which I'd forgotten about—that helped them in some special way.

I can't take all the credit for my Joanisms: They're borne from the people and experiences I've encountered that have made me a wiser and more robust person. I wish to thank everyone who has helped shape me. And to all of you reading this book, it is my honor to pass these Joanisms on to you.

Hardships can render us immobile, unable to make decisions or move forward. We feel trapped and boxed in. We get in the slumps. But even with all the challenges life presents us, we can enjoy growth and a journey of hope. I'm living proof!

My goal of this book is to lighten your load. To empower you to recognize that you can get through the most destructive earthquakes if you (a) take action; (b) drop, cover, and hold on; and then (c) emerge to rebuild an even sturdier castle, using a well-stocked toolbox.

I have learned the hard way to *live* well, *laugh* often, and *love* more. Death has taught me how to enjoy life to the fullest. Humor and light-hearted thinking are my survival tools. I am now happy and healthy, and I've gained a toughness that was unforeseeable in those bleak times. This has continued to help me through challenges, including caring for a mother with Alzheimer's and a sister with Down syndrome, obsessive-compulsive disorder, and Alzheimer's.

People ask me how I can be so positive. After losing a child, I recognize that the little stuff really is just little stuff. Let death inspire you to live!!!! I did!

1

FIFTY SHADES OF GREY

Whip Your Life Into Shape

What do my hair and Anastasia Steele from *Fifty Shades of Grey* have in common? My hairs have been lashed, flogged, and punished for my pleasure. I want them to be passive and pliant. They aim to please, but are at the same time rebellious and disobedient.

My hairs' ultimate revolt came in a grey-strand insurgence.

Spotting my first silver sentry standing guard, awaiting reinforcements amid the brown hairs fighting to survive, I instigated a complete overhaul of my problem hair. Paramount was finding the least expensive way to manage the unwanted on my head.

I called it the Affordable Hair Act.

A Plucker-Sucker

Peering into a magnifying mirror, I sent in the tweezers to yank out the stubborn suckers. Trauma rocked my world when the carnage in my sink showed more brown dead soldiers than grey. But snaking amongst the casualties was a *looooong* grey strand. Victory had been obtained.

Until I realized it was dental floss.

Declaring that battle lost, I paid my daughter to go in for the kill, believing this still cheaper than dying. She surrendered once she'd earned enough money to put a down payment on a house.

My grey-hair management was unmanageable.

I tried to seal up the problem with Gorilla Glue, but it seemed to just glob and spread. It did bond the greys to the browns, which is stylish if you're into that zebra motif.

Next, I dove into the Internet, but I chose to ignore the warnings that pulling out grey hairs might damage the follicles. (*And what might be wrong with that?* I reasoned.) Plucking seemed the only cheap solution—even if inhumane.

I've mastered the art, except a few problems. First, I can only see my grey hairs in front. For all I know, the back of my head looks like Eeyore's tail. And then I need a way to cover the bald spots where the collateral-damage brown hair used to proudly wave. My, this is getting expensive.

I have yet to resort to coloring my hair. But when I do, I'm going big and bold. Maybe bright red or purple. That seems the best way to lay the grey hairs to rest. That is, if I have any hair left by then.

MANEtaining My (Out)Look

I decided to leverage the Affordable Hair Act to manage other unwanteds in my life. I assembled a toolbox to MANEtain some control. Here are its essential items:

Affordable Hair Act
MANEtain Toolbox

1. **Magnifying Mirror** Focus in on the problem. Analyze the obstacle. Brainstorm how to handle the dilemma.
2. **Hairnet** Spread your net wide to gather available resources. Research your options and get varying viewpoints.
3. **Hairdresser** Communicate your wants, needs, and grievances—just like you do in your favorite beauty chair. Talk to a friend, the involved party, and/or a counselor.
4. **Battle Plan** Determine if the issue is spring-loaded, slow-growing, or an anomaly that will shed away with time. Plot out your offensive.
5. **Experiment Log** When ideas or processes fail, learn from the experience and record it to avoid repeating mistakes. After my first tweezing attempt, I learned not only that I needed a better method, but also to floss and pluck my hairs over two different sinks.
6. **Tweezers** Tackle the problem head on, kind of like popping a zit.

7. **Gorilla Glue** Stop the spread of the problem by setting boundaries and securing support from others. Your team can create simian-strength bonds that help you hold it together more cheaply and effectively than hair extension tape-ins. (After all, you want the problem to stop, not grow!)
8. **Hair Dye** If drastic measures are needed, embrace change: Move, switch jobs, take legal action.
9. **Waxing** Rip out a host of problems at once.
10. **Laser** Banish the problem forever.
11. **Brush and Blow** Guide your life in the direction you want it to go.
12. **Nothing** It's not always possible to manage your hair all the way from roots to ends. Carefree, loose waves are all the rage. And—hey!—sometimes if you can't see it, it's not a problem!

A Pus-Pocket Named Harold

When I was younger, it was men—not grey hairs—that were out of control. At age twenty-two, one doozy festering was named Harold: a hot-looking older man who seduced me with his good looks and charisma. We met in a college life-guarding class and he drowned me in his deceptions and dysfunctions. Like an unwanted hair, he was well-hung (in his case, that was actually part of the appeal), was one of many, showed up in all the wrong places, and needed to be plucked right out of my life.

But love at twenty-two is like a blind monkey on speed. There's a lot of confusion and you're sightless to the obvious. Your heart races, your libido increases, excessive howling ensues, and you cling to things that need to be let go of. I fell in love with Harold because of his animal magnetism: he was the most charming monkey hanging around. But in reality, he was an itchy, red ingrown hair—a puspocket that needed popping.

On our one-year anniversary, Harold and I met to celebrate; but instead of a luncheon, we found ourselves at Dysfunction Junction. At the beginning of our relationship, Harold had introduced me to his cousin, Olivia, with whom he was living. She looked like his cousin, acted like his cousin…she wasn't his cousin.

"I would like to make a toast," Harold announced as he raised his Pabst Blue Ribbon. "Roses are red, violets are blue, I love you, Joan, and Olivia, too…She is my wife, you are my life."

Say what???!!!

"How can that be?!" I cried. "You told me she was your cousin! And you wanted to make *me* your wife."

"I lied—I love her like a cousin," he smirked.

To me, sleeping with your girlfriend while living with your wife was like a humpback whale humping an orangutan: awkward and should be outlawed. But apparently not in this particular white-trash love nest.

Harold was a wild grey hair amongst the brown: sneaky, snake-like, and slick as dental floss. What I should have done was grab the tweezers from my MANEtain Toolbox and yanked that man and his so-called cousin right out of my life.

Instead, I said: "Well, okay…as long as you don't love her like you do me."

When it came to love, I was the role model for all blind monkeys on speed. Instead of brushing this hairbrain of a man aside, I made like a Rogaine-failed rug and stayed glued to him.

Baboon Harold liked to travel…to the liquor store and back. He swung from one job to another. He liked to eat everyone else's bananas instead of finding his own. Harold needed money, so I loaned him eight thousand dollars. He loved to read…my journal. So I used my Gorilla Glue and set boundaries. He tried to commit suicide.

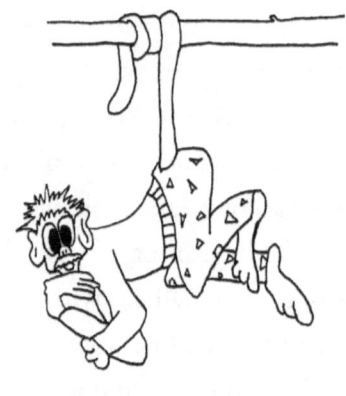

I took out my magnifying mirror and saw that this problem wasn't going away; it was getting bigger. I went to counseling. I broke up with him. When he wouldn't pay me back my money, I took him to small claims court and won.

I used a whole arsenal of tools to manage this situation: 1. **Magnifying Mirror**, 2. **Hairnet**, 3. **Hairdresser**, 4. **Battle Plan**, 6. **Tweezers**, 7. **Gorilla Glue**, 8. **Hair Dye**, and 10. **Laser**.

Harold is still alive, and to this day I'm using tool 5: **Experiment Log**. Harold was a learning experience I will never repeat.

Embrace the Greys & Pluck the Rest!

Do you have a swollen ingrown hair the size of Mount Vesuvius or a gaggle of greys springing up in your life? Maybe in the form of an unruly boss, a backstabbing friend, or a significant other who puts you down (or is in a relationship with their cousin)? Grab your MANEtain Toolbox and take control. Your actions are your pincers; your life-size Tweezerman.

And for the small stuff like traffic or long lines? Embrace your greys—accept what you cannot change. After all, grey is the new black. (Have you noticed the trend of young celebrities going grey on purpose? Though I still don't understand why the soundtrack for the *Fifty Shades of Grey* trailer is heavy breathing. Anyway…)

If you want to radiate full-color vibrancy in your life, say "pluck you" to those unwanted stressors. Tell them to *pluck off!* Go ahead—you can do it: *Pluck 'em.*

2

WHY I EAT MY YOUNG

Lessons Come in All Flavors

Stress can cause us to make bad decisions. Mine compelled me to resort to filial cannibalism.

But let me back up. The good decision I made was to take care of my sister, Lisa Jean—often referred to as L.J.—who has Down syndrome, OCD, *and* Alzheimer's, and my mother, also suffering from Alzheimer's. I am a Dagwood member of the sandwich generation: a group who cares for both their aging parents and their children. My Dagwood sandwich is piled high with responsibilities, spread too thin, and contains lots and lots of meat. It definitely fills my plate.

Due to L.J.'s government assistance, her care involves a superfluity of rules and regulations to sift through. I feel like a TV remote: there are too many instructions, my buttons are pushed way too often, and no matter how many options are selected, I am still surfing without results.

A Stress-Relief Snafu

L.J. was on a medication for five years before her situation attracted scrutiny from various agencies. One of the agencies assisting in her care management requested that I take her to a psych doctor to assure she was not exhibiting any side effects from the meds. You know: four horns, eleven toes, full head-spins, and drinking martinis after lunch. Oh, wait—those are *my* stress-related side effects.

This may not sound like much, but adding yet another doctor's appointment to our already-full regimen felt like being asked to carry a bucket full of rocks on my back from Kansas to Sri Lanka through places hotter than the devil's a-hole (known to PC-ers as the "devil's waste management area") where your mother sucks socks in hell.

So I wrote a letter to the agency. Then I hand-carried it to my sister's assisted-living meeting, held every six months to evaluate Lisa's goals, count her fingers and toes, make sure she was breathing, and basically ensure I wasn't smoking the socks from hell. Once we passed the test, she would continue to get funding, I would get more paperwork to fill out, and we would have more meetings at my mother and Lisa Jean's house, during which my mom would scare the heck out of people by telling them to leave as they walked in the door. Alzheimer's has no filter.

My plan was to discuss the letter with L.J.'s support team to see if there was any way around this extraneous evaluation. The group sat quietly as the meeting facilitator read my letter out loud so that they all could help me problem-solve.

December 18, 2013

To Whom It May Concern:

I, Joan Arent, co-guardian for L.J., request that L.J. not attend a psych evaluation for her Citalopram - 20mg, which she takes for anxiety. I do not feel this is time well spent, as her general practitioner, Dr. M., who prescribed it to assist her with her obsessive-compulsive disorder and the anxiety that results from the disorder, reviews this medication and her needs annually, or as needed.

I take L.J. and our mother, who has Alzheimer's, to most of their medical appointments. It is agitating to them both. These changes to the normal schedule are especially disruptive to L.J. due to her OCD. It stresses me out and makes me eat my young.

I feel we are managing her needs very well—in particular, her medication.

Sincerely,

Joan Arent

When the letter was done, silence fell on the room.

"Does this say it makes you eat your young?" the facilitator gasped.

I turned as many shades of pale as a Subway turkey sandwich on white bread with a motley array of mayo-like toppings—L.J.'s favorite meal—as my mind went through a good-cop/bad-cop battle in my brain.

Holy crap! my good cop thought. *I didn't mean for them to see that! What I wrote was an innocent stress reliever—a way to laugh at the challenges in my life. I hope I didn't offend anyone.*

Meanwhile, my bad cop defended: *Hell, yeah, it says that. I wrote it because that IS what this makes me feel like doing: eating my young and abolishing all requirements that cause me stress.*

In the end, neither cop talked. I did.

"Wait, uh, well, hmmm, yikes, yes, it does," I confessed.

The room erupted with laughter.

"I picked up this phrase," I explained, "when I asked a cashier at a very, very, *very* busy Whole Foods if the place was always like this. '*Yessss,*' he declared. 'It makes you eat your young.'

"I wrote that letter over a month ago," I went on, "when I was tired, stressed, and stretched to the limit by the demands put on me that don't always make a whole heck of a lot of sense. I had to add a little funny so as to not be so bitter. I planned to take that part out. I guess I forgot."

A Blunderful Lesson

This gaffe on my part led to my letter being copied and pinned to the office bulletin boards of all who had attended this meeting on Lisa Jean's behalf. Hanna, Kathy, Kris, Jane, and Nichole all have jobs that demand a lot and pay little. They do what they do for the love of working with people with disabilities who give back love unconditionally.

They also circulated my letter to colleagues to remind everyone to chuckle, to prevent "hardening of the attitudes."

At the next meeting for Lisa Jean, with seven people crowded into the small living room at her and Mom's house, Jane enlightened us all to the *Minions* term *snaughling: laughing so hard you snort, then laugh because you snorted, then snort because you laughed.* I wheeze and whinny for encores.

Blunders must be taken at face value. Have fun with them.

This particular blooper helped relieve the nervousness and tension of everybody. It was definitely one of those "I've never made a mistake…once I thought I did, but I was wrong" moments. I did make a mistake, but it wasn't wrong. It was a relief.

What blunder can you turn into a positive experience? How can that faux pas help you or others through the tough stuff?

Tool 12 of the MANEtain Toolbox can be used here: **Nothing.** Let it go; have fun with your mistakes. If something happens that you can't change, apologize, move forward, and be carefree. It's not possible to manage and control everything in your life. Don't take yourself too seriously.

By the way, I still had to take her to the psych doc. I brought my knife and fork.

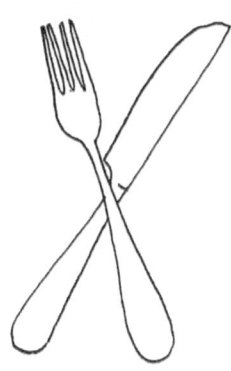

3

ROLL WITH IT

Sucking It Up to Survive

"Ten...nine...eight...seven...six...five...four...three...two..."
Survival being my first instinct, I tucked and rolled as the loud voice boomed overhead. Dropping my bag, I curled into fetal position and aimed for anyone who might get in the way of my living to see Oprah elected as President of the United States. Then I waited for a bomb to explode, a rocket ship to launch, or the entire crowd to be blown into kibble-sized bits of dog food.

Turns out, it was an automated warning that the crosswalk light in front of Terminal 2 at the San Diego airport was about to change.

How I would love to find the person who created this live-action Wii-game combat zone, laughing in Gollum's lair while recording a menacing countdown that shoots a bolt of adrenaline into the pedestrian who can't possibly figure out when it is safe to cross the street. I thought maybe a security alarm had gone off, having detected the thirteen inches of mesh sewn inside my belly.

Who knew I would have to "Roll With It" to withstand my imaginary fears? I half-expected Peyton Manning to yell "Omaha!" Wait…wasn't I in San Diego?

Roll With It is one of my mantras. No, I didn't say "Roll It"—though I am from Colorado, where that's a coping technique for many. What it means is that if you can't change the problem or have little control over it, then go with the flow. Don't fight it. But don't give up. Determine what is imaginary and what is real.

Burn, Baby, Burn

Tucking and rolling was not always an option for me, due to medical complications from the birth of my son, which for a long time remained a mystery. It would've been so much easier if I could have obviously blamed it on my six-pack stomach carrying triplets, or on Bob's coming out the size of the afore-mentioned Denver Broncos quarterback. But it started with an umbilical hernia, discovered a year after Bob's birth.

At the time, I was a fitness instructor. I taught aerobics and step until I was asked to stop teaching a week before Bob's due date; the club didn't want to have to find a sub at the last minute. I was so fit that the hernia did not create immediate issues, and medical advice was that if it wasn't bothering me, there was no need to repair it. So we didn't.

My problem arose four years later when I was struck by intense pain. A cyst burst like the atomic bomb. My six-pack stomach looked and felt like a dismal swamp. I could not sit, stand, or sleep without distress. I felt like a constipated Joey Chestnut, eleven-time champion of the annual Nathan's Hot Dog Eating Contest, who downed seventy-four dogs in ten minutes—including the buns. The trouble is, those puppies don't come out as easily as they go in.

Over nine *long* years of debilitating pain, I searched for an answer. I had MRIs, CAT scans, DOG scans, ultrasounds, strobe lights, and Easter egg dye injected into me until I looked like a Smurf. I saw acupuncturists, internal medicine specialists, my family doctor, my family doctor's family doctor, two gastrologists, and a naturopathic doctor.

"I think this is all in your head," one doc told me. "Have you ever considered a lobotomy?"

"Why, yes," I replied. "That and lighting myself on fire while singing *'Burn, baby, burn, disco inferno.'*"

Bulging bloodshot eyes, hair shooting out in thirty-four thousand directions, clenched teeth, flaring nostrils, vice-grip jaw...no this is not me before coffee. This is a black-and-white drawing I gave to my homeopath with the caption: *I have one nerve left. Please don't get on it.*

My next stop was a witch doctor in Uganda. He had that jungle magnetism every girl in physical agony longs for. But he couldn't find my one nerve because the homeopath had gotten on it.

I continued my quest to escape from my own private torture chamber by going to five different physical therapists. I saw a specialist in muscle issues and a specialist of a specialist of a specialist. I was told not to eat gluten, dairy, soy, nuts, large mammals such as killer whales, or fur-covered animals.

One PT used mini jumper cables to jump-start body parts that I didn't know could handle that much electric current. I visited a sex shop to buy tools to decrease the pain—doctor's orders, no kidding. I saw a pelvic pain specialist, who gave me drugs that caused so many side effects I asked, "How much suffering do I need to do to stop suffering?" Shoot your foot to forget the pain in your back.

Celebrating summer solstice, I mingled with the rich and rambunctious partygoers who did drugs of many colors—but not of the kind needed to calm the angry beast ripping me apart from the inside. As I nibbled on a cracker with the texture of Astroturf, free of all dietary demons and flavor, a dashingly debonair man sauntered up to me.

"Hellooooo," he said.

"Charmed," I growled.

"You are stunning," he lied.

"You too," I didn't lie.

"Have you ever had Botox?" he inquired.

"Why, yes," I answered in a silky voice, "in my stomach."

He walked away.

Gnaw, Nibble, and Ride

Roll With It works like this: Visualize being on a bike. My torment was so bad that all I could do was imagine riding past the obstacles (in my case, the pain). I traveled around the rocks (my disappointment over so many medical tests leading to still no answers), over the roots (my lack of sleep), through the piranha-infested rivers (the doctors who told me I was crazy, or the ones who got mad at me for seeing more than one specialist).

Let others' negativity roll off you like seagull slop off a bald surfer's head.

I heed this advice when working with difficult people. The coordinator at a soup kitchen gave similar guidance when a homeless man said to the ten-year-old handing him his meal: "White boys burn in hell." Not exactly the thank-you the boy was expecting. But no harm done, especially if he could *Roll With It* by realizing that this man had issues and his comment wasn't personal.

I imagined my dilemma as pizza dough. Nobody said I couldn't eat *that*. I plopped it on the table. I got distance from it. I kneaded it, pounded it, and stretched it, and it remained manageable. I could share it with others; people aren't afraid of pizza. It was something I could snack on, bit by bit. I refrigerated it—out of sight, out of mind. Sort of.

Cookie dough can be chunky and sticky and chewy. Look at the situation as one you can enjoy, conquer, and gnaw through. Savor it and enjoy it with a glass of milk. The issue can be multidimensional, like a friendship or family relationship. Family can be sticky, since it is not a bond you can easily let go of. And it is often chunked with different personalities, age groups, and backgrounds. Slow down and nibble at the dough.

Focus on problem-solving, moving forward, and the trail of obstacles ahead. Think of ways to get through them. Consider what tools you have: your gears, your protective helmet, your water for replenishing. When things get rocky, look around the rocks, look over the rocks, or simply sit back and hold on tight, having faith you can get to your destination—your final goal. Mine was to live pain-free.

Ever Enmeshed

Today, I live pain-free.

After so many years of searching for answers, my fourth ultrasound showed that my abdominal wall was tearing due to the umbilical hernia. *Hallelujah!*

However, it took yet another year to figure out how to remedy the issue. A dear longtime friend who's a physical therapist is the one who proposed surgery as a possible solution. The surgeon didn't even know if it was going to help, but I was desperate.

Victory came as those thirteen inches of mesh pulled my life together. Of course, I won the prize for being one of the rare women in the world who suffers an inguinal hernia as a side effect of surgery for an umbilical hernia. I had to undergo more surgery to repair the complications from the surgery before.

I was scratched, bruised, tired, fitter, stronger, energized, and more experienced—better equipped to conquer the next adventure life put in front of me.

After my mesh surgery, the full-body scanners at airports always think I swallowed a fishing net. I have to be careful swimming; I catch a lot of suckerfish.

Thanks to the latticework in my belly, I can tuck and roll my way through any problem, imagined or real. Like Peyton Manning, I'm good under pressure. Maybe I'll even start shouting "Omaha!"

4

JOANIE IN A LAMP

Shifting Your Poo-spective

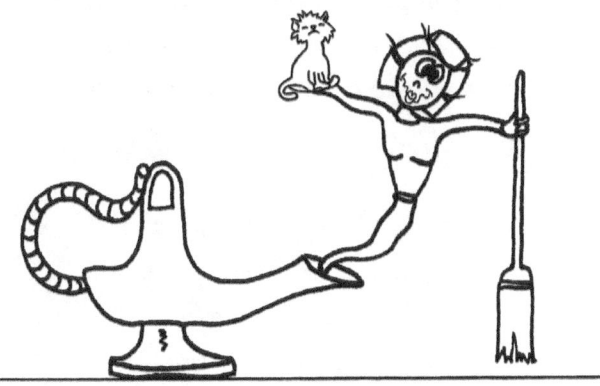

I feel like a genie in a lamp.

One who is often rubbed the wrong way—which I suppose is true of any other spouse, parent, business owner, caregiver, sibling, and person who has GAS (more on that in Chapter 14!).

As a mother of two children, I'm not always my own master. It's a good thing I'm not fastidious, because this job would be hideous. My "itty-bitty living space" is cluttered with toys, dirty socks, underwear, cat spew, gerbil poo, and dog burps resembling *The Book of Mormon* musical: colorful and distasteful.

I'VE NEVER MADE A MISTAKE...

I wish I could limit everyone in my life to three wishes. But *noooo*, I have to change a poopy diaper, find the head of the Jurassic World Lego Dilophosaurus (sometimes *I* dream of being extinct), search out the toilet plunger, arrange medical appointments for four people (not including my own needed sanity check), and prepare meals to stifle the pathetic wails of "I'm starving!" from my husband, the neglected breadbasket.

Out I pop from the lamp, and suddenly I am Joanerella. I've got Disney mice singing: *"Every time she finds a minute, that's the time when they begin it!"*

I make up my own verses:

> *Joanerelly, Joanerelly—night and day, it's Joanerelly!*
> *"Make the breakfast, fix the remote,*
> *clean the fish tank, don't rock the boat.*
> *Be my plaything, do the Swiffing—*
> *and the heavy-lifting.*
> *Joanerelly, do the shopping!"*
> *They always keep me hopping!*
> *I go around in circles*
> *'til I'm in a great big tizzy.*
> *Still, they holler, "Keep a-busy, Joanarelly!"*

I see no party dress in this for me.

The mice and I are trapped in a multitasking maze with a loooong to-do list, an even longer wish list, and breaks as short as the pluck of an unwanted nose hair.

If I *were* in a Walt Disney movie, the artist would draw my body to resemble a dipstick because I enter into sticky situations from which I sometimes cannot exit cleanly—like when one-year-old Anna (sound asleep from a swig of cough syrup) peed on me during a flight to Europe. I had of course packed a change of clothes for her but not me. I'd have a wire whip for a head because I must whip things up in a hurry: school projects, mac 'n' cheese, gourmet dog food-and-pill concoctions for our incontinent family member, Twitch. I would have a broom for feet to clean up all the messes—both real and metaphorical—and a life preserver around my waist, for my job of helping keep people afloat (while at times sinking myself).

At the end, Prince Charming would run me over with a MINI Cooper, seeing it as an act of heroism for putting me out of my misery.

My Fight to Stay Abreast of My Tit-uation

The phone rings. It's my health insurance company, apparently assuming my breasts are just hanging around with nothing to do. (Well, they *are* hanging around, but they are not idle.) The agent is calling to tell me that my insurance covers only fifty percent of my mammogram and would I like to have both breasts covered by paying an additional fee?

"Are you serious?" I ask. "Insurance will cover only one of my breasts? Are you asking me to choose which breast's life I'm willing to gamble with?"

"We can only cover half the bill," he repeats.

I feel like I'm in a high-stakes poker game. Yes, I'd like to stack my deck: I'll raise you two breasts for one kidney and a bladder. I ask the scheduler if he would like to be my Seven Card Stud and play this hand with me. There is going to be a showdown at the Sally Jobe Imaging Office. The two cards to be dealt are my breasts; it would be nice if I had a Texan to hold 'em.

I then tell the man with a straight poker face that, instead, I will check my own breasts for lumps with my son's light saber. But there will not be Obi-*One* because I have two to consider.

Tweet, tweet! A text whistles at me like I'm a dog, telling me I have an appointment for my llama to be trimmed. I don't have a llama…do I?

Out I run to the grocery store. I try to rejoice in the celebration printed on my six breasts: *YOU SAVED 30% ON THIS PACKAGE!* I'm referring to chicken, but hmmm…could I tell the insurance agent I have six breasts, so that they'll cover three?

I connive a plan to knock off my demanding dinner guests who just won't let me rest—*Joanerelly! Joanerelly!* I ask the Safeway fish lady named Waterfront (at least that's what her apron says), "Which is more poisonous: the pollution in the wild-caught salmon or the preservatives in the farm-raised salmon? Or perhaps you have some 'spine-on' Filipino blowfish? I'm more than willing to pay market price."

Shifting and Spritzing

I imagine myself as a shapeshifter from *Star Trek 6*—you know the characters that can change themselves into anyone they want? The problem is I am actually a "shit-shifter," moving the dirty laundry into the washer, transplanting the cat puke from the carpet to the trash, introducing the chicken to the salmon…all while shifting my perspective accordingly.

No, Mrs. Crabapple, I don't mind dropping everything because Bob has locked himself in the bathroom at school. No, Mrs. Crabtree, I don't mind exiting my Jazzercise class because Anna has flipped off another first-grader. No, I don't mind eating mac 'n' cheese instead of going out to dinner at the Ritz with Prince Charming because he has to work late. I'll just take off my glass slippers and drink swamp juice out of them.

I was feeling erotic; now I'm headed for psychotic.

Shit-shifting can work in your favor with the help of your own version of poo-pourri: a product that sprays away the crappy stenches in one's life. When mother lodes of dung drop down and stink up your world, spritz your way from sour thoughts to more fragrant ones. Find the humor in your poo of a problem.

Singing for Sanity

When my children were little, I called them "PITAs." They never knew it stood for Pains In The Ass. I created a song for my two-year-old when he cried for forty minutes as we drove to pick up some tea:

Sung to the tune of "I'm a Little Teapot"

I'm a little kid, short and stout
Make me mind and hear me shout.
When I get all steamed up,
I just pout.
Make me mind and I will flout!

I am a special boy—yes, it's true.
Here's an example of what I can do:
I can spin my head around and spout,
kick my legs, and scream and glout.

Make me mind and you'll have your doubts
that I'm a little kid, short and stout.

If you can't change it, then rearrange it or flush it down the toilet. Don't stay trapped in a porcelain prison.

You know there is no such thing as a poo-fect life. Everyday demands can be tenacious and you can't control what bricks might drop. But your poo-pourri—your shifting of viewpoint—can help you find a poo-spective that works in your favor. It can also rid you of the fetor, the bark burp, the cat barf, and the gerbil doo-doo.

When life rubs you the wrong way and you feel like a Joanie in a Lamp, remember: You *do* have the power of a genie. You have magic in your world, fired by endless mental possibilities. No more prairie-dogging your problems away.

5

DON'T SLEEP WITH FABIO

Put Your Stress to Rest

N aked, I lie exposed to the damp air, heavy with a wetness of its own making. Bathed in sweat, I seek solace from the relentless, unforgiving realities of my life. Besieged by anger, bitterness, and sorrow, I find glimpses of relief in the dense, dark fog I call sleep.

A firm presence penetrates my being, stimulating my senses with the suggestive touch of his sticky Herculean manliness. Currents of familiarity reverberate through my body like shock waves of an electrical storm, heightening my senses, pricking my skin, and jolting my mind to attention. He slides between the sheets and whispers seductively: "Sleep is not yours to have."

As his breath skates across my neck, each hair frolics in a dance of desire, reaching for his touch. He brusquely pulls me closer, arousing me with the heat of his tan, chiseled torso. He is a god sculpted from pure naughtiness. The titillating scent of his passion torments me—I am teased by what I want but can't have.

His penetrating eyes, dark and smoky, draw me in like a deep pool of cool water.

"Come to me, I want you," he purrs.

His words are like melted butter: thick, warm, and clinging to me, begging me to surrender to his wants—not mine. He is arrogant. I can feel his heart pulsating, his heat rising. I am suffering in my thirst to be satiated.

He misunderstands my moans as hunger for him. I push him away.

"Stop, I don't want you!" I whimper. "All I want is sleep—and maybe a banana."

Sleep is the orgasm I am seeking. But my uncontrolled thoughts, seductively tantalizing, haunt me in the form of my  imaginary mental mate I call Fabio. He is the foreplay I don't desire.

An Open Orgy

Night after night, my mind fights the urge to stray. Fabio is not attractive; he makes me restless and stressed. He controls me like Christian in *Fifty Shades of Grey*. I pretend he is Grey's brother—but far more seductive and dangerous because he doesn't need whips and chains; he does it all with the power of suggestion.

I can't resist. He tumbles between the sheets whether I'm alone or not. I have no self-control. So little that I then let all sorts of other sleep seducers crawl under the covers and into my mind. Freddy, my real-life nightmare who owes me money; Anastasia, my employee who can't seem to understand that a deadline is a deadline—especially when it comes to solving a murder; Collin, my seventh web designer (at least he didn't go to jail like my first one); and Dr. Woodcock, who tried to help me banish my sexy insomnia sweetheart with form after form after form to fill out for medical clarity. These people are the stressors in my life, providing enough strain to keep my mind racing. They are happy to join me in bed, even when I try drastic measures to keep them out: meditation, prayer, a swig of wine, music, a cup of hot milk, sometimes even drugs. Half a Tylenol PM is a drug, right?

We lie there for hours mulling over the Murders and Acquisitions case we are working on. *Freddy, Freddy, Freddy.* He justifies why he can't pay me. He needs his beer-pong ping-pong table, his beaver fur coat (which is really groundhog fur), and his donation to save the pink fairy armadillo. Collin offers excuse after excuse for why it is going to cost way more than planned to make that itty-bitty change to my website to make me millions. Dr. Woodcock has only apologies, which I'll take.

While my self-restraint is nonexistent, my mental foes go on hikes with me, travel with me, and eat dinner with me, all uninvited.

The Power of S & M (Sleep & Meditation)

To sleep with Fabio is not to sleep. I emailed Fabio to take control, to set my boundaries:

> **From:** Mary Dew Furrybush
> **Subject:** Assault and Battery of My Mind
> **Date:** February 14, 2:00 a.m.
> **To:** Fabio Grey

I'VE NEVER MADE A MISTAKE...

Dear Mr. Fabio,

I know you are not real. You are only the accumulation of the stressors in my life, joining me in my thoughts when I want you the least: in my bed. I feel spanked, invaded, and punished for the challenges of my days. I am not aroused. Have you tried therapy for your stalker tendencies? I need help ridding you of my life, at least when the lights go out.

Thank you,
Mary Dew Furrybush

From: Fabio Grey
Subject: Free Your Mind or Find Your G-Spot
Date: February 14, 11:00 a.m.
To: Mary Dew Furrybush

Dear Mary Dew,

Take control. You have the power to manage me. Think of it as mind masturbation. Find your G-spot. Your Go-to-sleep spot. Close your eyes and imagine a point in your mind; that is your G-spot. Focus on that. Breathe in and breathe out; meditate on one word, any word, and repeat the breathing and the word over and over until you fall asleep.

You could repeat my name over and over—it has a nice meditative ring to it. *Grrrr...Fabio, gggggrrrr... Faaaaabio, grrrr...Fabbbio. Inhale, exhale.* If that doesn't work, pray and think of rabbits in Nebraska. Imagine your life as a sloth. Think of me as a bed bug, and smack, pick, and flick me out from under the covers. Dictate to Siri; she is always there for you. Practice your G-spot exercise during the day; this makes you more powerful at night. Imagine your thoughts bound and gagged and your body free of me.

GO TO SLEEP!!!
Fabio Grey

I can control Fabio. After all, he just told me how to do it without whips and chains. Excuse me while I go masturbate my mind.

6

A TALE OF THREE POOL BOYS

Just Keep Swimming

I asked for a pool boy for my birthday: sculpted, boosterish, bronzed, buffed, and devoted to all my liquid needs. As my cabana concierge, he would dote on me, fan me, and whet my palette with refreshments. He wouldn't talk, as that would mean he would have an opinion. I don't mind hearing opinions as long as they are mine.

I didn't get a pool boy for my birthday but I did get to watch one unwrap himself. My ideal pool boy came into my life in the most unexpected way. In fact, I have enjoyed three pool boys.

Pool Boy #1

The first pool boy was a hot, muscular, Magic Mike–type, who was visiting San Diego from Australia with his mate. We met at an evening work party. He was crashing the event; I was not. We chatted, we laughed, we shared cultural stories. When most of the guests had left, he asked if it might be okay to swim.

"You think anyone would mind?" he enquired.

"Nah!" I assured him. "Why would anyone mind?"

He smiled; I smiled. He peeled off his shirt and dropped his drawers; I dropped my jaw. He plunged in with his skivvies on. It was the best unwrapping job I had ever seen.

Two tipsy women, stunned by the dark beauty gracing their otherwise boring night, gave up all rights to calling themselves mature, intelligent, responsible adults and drooled on their evening finery as their gazes followed the eye candy into the pool.

A security guard with no sense of adventure halted the pair's impending swan dives by gruffly announcing: "Sir, you aren't allowed to swim. This is a private party."

The ladies whimpered and whined. I grabbed a towel and my pool boy wrapped it around himself.

"He's with me," I said.

Pool Boy #2

This one showed up in Arizona on a very, very hot day. I said hello to the aging-like-fine-wine worker as he was checking the chlorine levels at my hotel's pool.

He replied by saying, "Today is a *gooooooood* day."

"That it is," I agreed.

The next day, I greeted him again.

"Today is a *gooooooood* day," he told me again.

"Do you say that every time someone says hello?" I asked.

"Yes," he explained. "Years and years ago, when I was working outside in 115 degree heat, I was cranky and very uncomfortable. I knew I had to change my perspective to keep doing my job. So I did."

That was his solution to managing a tough reality. Instead of complaining, he turned the negative into the positive. He was hot, hot, hot in a different way.

Pool Boy #3

While imitating a lobster, in a hot tub in Snowmass, Colorado, I started conversing with the third pool boy. He was skimming the water for leaves and bugs. He shared that he had moved from Hawaii to Colorado because his wife had gotten a great job promotion. I applauded his relocation and his support for his wife.

"I'm just happy to be alive," he told me. He divulged that he had volunteered at a hospice for five years and explained how that experience had enlightened him to appreciate every single day.

Pool Your Resources

Just keep swimming to find the pool boy of *your* dreams and the wisdom and knowledge that can come in many different shapes and sizes.

The Dalai Lama, God, and Oprah could learn a few things from these pool boys. I wonder what *those* three look like in their skivvies?

7

A BITCH, A BITCH

Life's a Bitch—Enjoy It

Some were thin as lampposts, others round as sumo wrestlers. Bedecked in floral-and-checked garments reminiscent of my favorite curtains, their luscious skin was as smooth as pumpkins and as inky as dark chocolate. My children and I—the "Mzungus" with toilet-paper-hued complexions—were blinding next to them.

But these ladies' most valuable asset was their ability to find joy in a storm of sorrow.

I'VE NEVER MADE A MISTAKE...

The rainbow-glass-sharded walls surrounding us stank worse than the urinals in Dodger Stadium, were topped with barbed wire that would make *matoke* out of any intruder's dumb ass, and were protected by men with guns the size of large children. The dust cloud swirling around us made the place a fantasyland for Charlie Brown's buddy Pig-Pen.

My kids, Bob and Anna, and I were volunteering in a makeshift classroom set up in a parking lot in Jinja, Uganda. We had come in the hopes of changing these women's lives. They were the ones who changed us.

Profiles in Poverty and Perseverance

Santa, like the others, speaks no English. Her mother tongue is Luo. She lives in a dilapidated home crafted from sticks and mud that even the Big Bad Wolf wouldn't waste his breath on. Her profession is moonshine production. If the distillery next to her house blew up, it would make the atomic bomb look like my twelve-year-old's science project gone bad. She talks about finding another way to make a living because hers attracts the village elite—the drunks and plunderers—but this is one of the easier ways to feed her six children and eight other dependents. Funny, I'd have thought one of her three husbands would have wanted to help out with that.

Adda Beatrice is a widow who wishes she could have died in the war she escaped from in Northern Uganda. She watched as rebels beheaded her husband. Subsisting on a dollar a day, she can't always afford food and owns six pieces of clothing. She lives in fear of disease, starvation, and rape.

Caynee Rose hid in the bushes from rebels for three days, with her children, along with the children of her siblings who died as a result of the war. She and her family moved with nothing but the clothes on their back. She is now the sole provider for her own five children, her sister's six children, and her brother's four children. Apparently word got out that she was living in luxury in her cozy ten-by-five-foot, no-bed, no-bath, airy outdoor kitchen, wall-to-wall dirt carpet, open-floor-plan dwelling with a TV. The slums have no electricity for it, but, hey, you can't have everything.

Through the help of Outreach Uganda—the organization we were volunteering with—these ladies make beads, bracelets, and bangles to sell in the United States to supplement their dollar-a-day income and pay for their children's education. Along with eighty-two other joyful women, they roll very thin strips of magazine pages into beads.

Hmmm…I should try to get these ladies jobs rolling joints at a pot facility—they'd be fantastic. And they would probably be immune to the fumes because they're already used to dunking their beads in shellac and hanging them to dry in their ten-by-five living spaces for three days. And let me tell you: those vapors would make Bob Marley roll over in his grave.

Anna and I taught daily classes on product development and color design. Bob created a mini-documentary. Anna also taught English and computer classes.

But my children were learning as much as they were teaching.

Some women would walk five to ten miles each morning from the very poorest areas of Jinja, Masese, Danida, Soweto, and Walukuba to come to our classes, leaving their nine-year-olds in charge of their other dependents at home ranging from ages one to eight. The women would attend classes all day, go to work for another four hours, and then walk home.

Clapping Shut the Communication Gap—With One Hand

Santa asked via a translator: "Why is Joan's hair like string from the mat I sleep on?"

"Why doesn't Bob have ten children?" Adda Beatrice inquired.

Bob responded with a loooooong, low whistle. He was only seventeen.

Caynee Rose wanted to know: "How can I get those teeth decorations Anna has?" Anna's "teeth jewelry," priced at over three thousand dollars, could have bought Caynee Rose:

1. The Heifer Foundation
2. Her own pool boy
3. Old Spice, so that her man who doesn't help pay the bills or support the children could smell like the Old Spice Man
4. The Old Spice Man—maybe he could help pay the bills

The language of hand signals, body wiggles, Elvis Presley gyrations, and high-fives closed the communication gap—and that was just *me* talking. I looked like I had ants in my pants, had just won the Super Bowl and was going to Disneyland, and was a three-year-old trying not to pee my Batman underwear.

All the women loved my high-fives. I would run around and give each of them a welcoming slap as they sat on their grass mats in heat so hot you could punch it.

Like the gorillas and chimpanzees we'd seen on our visit, I resorted to sounds and high leaps, splayed fingers, and celebratory hand-smacking to applaud Ajek Oorana for her beautiful jewelry design; Margaret Ekwaar for arriving on time to class rather than on "Africa time" (which would have had her gracing us with her presence at bedtime); and Adeth Betty for not making me eat the roasted ants she had laid out for a snack.

A Bitch, A Bitch

As I was performing my antics, in particular the high-fives, the women would chant what sounded like *"A Bitch, A Bitch."* They were in fact saying "a beech, a beech," which in Luo means "a five, a five." The results were laughter, improved self-esteem, personal growth, experiential learning, and awe-inspiring progress: The women were more confident, more accepting of their new role in a country that proclaimed the man the leader, but in which that same man would not provide for his family, and clearer about what steps to take to succeed

It also resulted in my new label for life.

Of all the nicknames I have been called, *A Bitch, A Bitch* has found its way into my personal Guinness Book of Titles I immediately respond to. My dog, Twitch, has shown signs of jealousy; she thought the name denoted her honorary position of power as the alpha female in the house.

Granted, I am called *A Bitch, A Bitch* for other reasons that I'm sure my siblings would be happy to share. As would the lady at the clothing store who didn't like that I had a newborn and looked as thin as Sleeping Beauty with a breast reduction.

A Bitch, A Bitch started with one small gesture and has become my sobriquet for life. It has taken on a meaning of its own.

The Ultimate Swimming Lesson

Two years later, I returned to Uganda with a friend who had been lured by the grasshopper popcorn snacks and the machete-wielding guard at the hotel we stayed at. She was especially excited to have rats visit as she huddled under the netting protecting her from mosquitoes the size of 747s. We went to the same school to teach a business class. The ladies still called me *A Bitch, A Bitch*.

I schooled them on American fashion via an *InStyle* magazine, apologizing for the photos of Paris Hilton's shoe closet—explaining that no, we Americans don't all have closets the size of Olympic swimming pools. Their response: "What's a swimming pool?"

From there, I didn't bother with a lesson on what a closet was—they didn't have enough clothes, shoes, or space for a closet. But we did take them on a field trip to a hotel swimming pool.

First we had to get them into swimsuits. The thin ones, we safety-pinned into tank suits we had brought along. For those with Volkswagen Bug–sized curves, we bought them slinky polyester lingerie to wear. They embraced their size with humor, dignity, and pride. In Uganda, to be large is to be loved. All the women wore shower caps to protect their delicate locks.

Your life flashes before you when a hippopotamus-sized woman in a floral-motif slip who has never even seen a pool, much less learned how to swim, dives toward you to commandeer you as her very own personal floatation device in three feet of water. Lifesaving is a skill I have since put on my résumé; I'm talking about my own life.

Visualize these ladies in the Miss Universe pageant strutting the runway in their makeshift swimwear worn over their Ugandan flag–inspired girdles and bras. We didn't have the heart to tell them that swimsuits are worn with nothing underneath.

Although these ladies had so little, it took even less to make them happy. They taught me to be positive in hard times. I learned it's not what I have but whom I surround myself with that's important. And that no matter how difficult I think my life is, I have it very, very, very good.

I am forever in these women's debt because they taught me to stand strong. Like dignified trees, they are rooted against forces of nature that swirl around, beat upon, and test them daily. No matter how harsh their realities are, they reach toward the sun, continuing to achieve growth through the rays of warmth and the drops of dew that sustain them.

They thanked my children and me by giving us our very own yellow, orange, and blue computer-microchip-patterned pantsuits (one size fits all) and making me one of their official sisters. I am honored to be called Sister *A Bitch, A Bitch*.

But, wait! In Uganda, when a woman marries, the husband-to-be has to give the woman's family a cow or a chicken, or if she is extra special, a goat or maybe a dog. As *A Bitch, A Bitch* nobody's going to barter *me* as a bride. My bite is worse than my bark, and these grooms wouldn't know what bit them!

8

ELIZA, ELIZA

Gone But Not Forgotten: Lessons in the Unseen

Dark hair like tufts of rabbit fur sit on your head like a winter cap. Your face is formed from the air that would not come, black and blue from fighting so hard for a life that was not yours to have.

You longed to reach our open arms, to *be*, to shape a history for all to embrace—to provide memories to cling to when you were no longer. You shouted to me in a dream: *"Listen, I am here! Something is wrong. Please help me."*

Your first cry is silent. Your breath holds no air.

Wait—watch her. She is taking her first steps. She has the power to BE. Her giggle so sweet, you scoop her in the air and celebrate. Those strides lead her to scraped knees, first love, graduation day, her twenty-first birthday, grandchildren, and a map of wrinkled skin etched in a face that has seen so much but in reality experienced nothing.

On December 23, 1994, you slipped away and left us with the gift of what-ifs. For nine months, you lived in your world and strained to honor us with those memories that weren't to be—no wedding dress or soft caress.

I watched you grow and felt your bumps and wiggles telling me you were not to be forgotten. Yet, toward the end, even those became weak taps, like a miner trapped in a coal mine as oxygen escaped his final grasp. Exhausted, you surrendered to the battle waged in the only home you knew: my belly. I was your door to something unknown. Your death was the slamming of my heart.

Hello and Good-Bye

Friends and family gathered in a winterland of solace to say good-bye to you, having never had the chance to say hello.

Bundled in a coat, snow mittens, and sorrow I sang, "If you're happy and you know it, clap your hands!", a song I would have sung to you had I held you in my arms.

Your father read a poem written by our dear friend Frank:

Eliza, Eliza

Eliza, Eliza,
Who might you have become?
No, better the question you beckon
from beyond our conscious questions:
Who are you?

Eliza, Eliza

You, too, shout mutely
not "I was,"
not "I would have been,"
but "I AM! I AM! I AM!"

"*I AM! I AM, I AM HERE WITH ALL OF YOU!*" Eliza yells in a hushed roar. I hear you loud and clear. Eliza you *are*, yet forgotten. As a stillborn child you are *still* in people's memories, left behind because you did not create tangibles for people to rejoice in and embrace. Overlooked in others' eulogies, the words not written: "Along with Peter, David, and Karen, Eliza died before her grandmother."

Your last breath was before your birth. You slipped away before we had a chance to know you. We reach for you and you are not there.

Eliza, Eliza,
Yet blessed with an eternal present.
Which present you now give to us,
and give, and give, and give.
Have you simply left our world,
or have you enlarged it to encompass
and be encompassed by your own?

Life After Death

Your loss hit me with the force and velocity of a meteorite. Impressions of you ripple through each person I encounter, like a gentle breeze driven by a mysterious gale. It reshaped me like waves against the shore, one grain of sand at a time.

As Michelangelo said: "No thought exists in me which death has not carved with his chisel." Your death is the paintbrush in my hand guiding the pigment, creating memories and images of their own on the canvas of my life.

Your eternal rest is affirmed in the lessons I have learned, the tears I have shed, and my compassion for others who have lost. The pain that reverberates and echoes to the depths of my soul because I *do* understand their hurt, shock, and confusion as they grieve the loss of a child, a relationship, a loved one. You gave me the power of empathy to be a life preserver for people like Amanda who lost her young son Paul.

"Joan," Amanda told me, "I listen to the words 'When Eliza died' roll off your tongue, without it catching your breath or ripping out your guts. I hope I will someday find the same strength to say that tortuous utterance: 'When my son Paul died' without it wrenching out my heart and exposing the raw emotions I felt the moment it happened."

Your death enrolled me in a club I never wanted membership in. It qualified me to be a compass to those who involuntarily join this community of loss, afloat in a magnitude of emotions.

Amongst feelings of such high intensity, one's sense of self is like a small craft adrift in a tsunami that has pitched them against cliffs of shock, confusion, and anger, screaming "Why? Why? Why?" I am but one anchor in the sea of their pain, offering hope despite loss, faith in times of disbelief, and trust that this agony of such force will not swallow them whole and that calmer waters of peace and healing lie ahead.

Your gift is all the lives you have touched not through memories of you but in the person I have become.

Your passing is the wind beneath my wings that keeps me soaring, celebrating what I have because you are gone. Your muted cry is the "why" behind my intense love for my children, my husband, my family, and my friends. Your silent heartbeat whispers guidance of love, laughter, and forgiveness. You have taught me that each day is a gift, each life an honor, and that each second holds the potential to be the last.

I am no longer innocent; I am stronger. I am no longer naïve; I am smarter. I am no longer lost; I am found.

You have taught me to live life because of your loss.

Eliza, Eliza
You who were, and are, and ever shall be.
We hear your muted cry—
though in truth, ours is much louder:
"I AM!"

9

CABBAGE PATCH KIDDIE BREASTS

Find Your Buddies

When one develops breasts, the hope lies in a round, voluptuous set like Halle Berry's or Scarlett Johansson's. When such wishes don't come true, one focuses on the positives of having Cabbage Patch Kiddie Breasts (CPKBs):

- You don't need protective eyewear during exercise to avoid breast-blinding by your super-size mammary melons.

- You save mega-money by not having to purchase over-the-shoulder boulder holders.

- You get to have meaningful conversations with eye-to-eye contact, rather than shallow tête-à-têtes (or tit-to-tits) with your snuggle pups.
- Your headlights aren't always on high beam.
- You pay less for a mammogram. (I assume this is another reason my insurance company only offered to pay fifty percent!)

No matter which way your boobs flop, it's breast to be happy with what you have.

A Recipe for Release

Who knew that after Eliza died I would have a real-life cabbage patch on my CPKBs?

When you have a stillborn child, your body believes incorrectly that you have an infant to take care of and it responds accordingly. Eliza had been a week overdue; my hormones were amuck. I carried twenty extra pounds, and overnight my hips morphed from gridiron goalposts to Free Willy. The ol' bait-and-switch especially confused my two breast friends, my *muchachas*, which still wanted to feed a baby.

"To avoid your breast milk coming in," the nurse had instructed us, "place *cool raw* cabbage on your breasts. Do this daily until the swelling stops and the breast milk retreats." Having just lost a child, however, Allen and I had not retained her helpful recipe.

Dolly Parton made her way into my over-the-shoulder pebble holders, as did the pain of having engorged gourds. This was one boob job gone bad. And it started on Christmas Day.

What to do, what to do? Did she say rutabaga fried with a reduction sauce? Or was it Brad Pitt's warm hands swathed in coconut oil?

Cabbage Patch Kiddie Breasts

Yuletide season meant all those schooled in breast-downsizing were off in winter hinterlands. So we sought advice from those we felt would be the most knowledgeable.

The somewhat correct recipe is as follows:

> **Cabbage Patch Kiddie Breast Milk Reduction**
>
> INGREDIENTS
> 1 head of green cabbage
> 2 boneless breasts
> 5 teaspoons of patience
> 10 cups of love
> 5 cloves of a sense of humor
> 3/4 teaspoon of salt
>
> INSTRUCTIONS
> Boil cabbage.
> Add sense of humor, patience, love, and salt.
> Reduce heat. Cook until cabbage is tender.
> Remove from heat. Cool and freeze cabbage.
> Place frozen cooked cabbage on CPKBs.
> Wait for Dolly Parton imposters to shrink.
> Repeat for 5 days.

As I blanketed my now double-Ds in solid crystallized cabbage-packs, I watched the icy blast create frozen fractals around my already violated milk containers. I cried because I was being reduced to a cabbage patch. I wept because I finally had Marilyn Monroe twin sisters and I didn't want them, and I had lost my daughter, Eliza. I laid back and waited for breast reduction to begin.

My Breast Supporters

How to Win Friends and Influence People was not the book I was reading while my Antarctica high ridges receded like glaciers affected by global warming. Frozen cooked cabbage thaws like plastic melting on a hot furnace. So I reeked like a dead skunk as the cabbage liquefied. As Dolly Parton retreated, leaving me with frozen butter twins, *my family* also retreated—to the far end of the house.

My son sought solace from Twitch, as the dog smelled better than I did. Meanwhile, Twitch laid around hoping for an epicurean meal of breast and cabbage.

I slept on a Slip 'N Slide to avoid the dripping cabbage juice making soup on my bed. At least I had a bit of fun in this process. I wish I could say that I watched the movie *Frozen*, finding comfort in relating to Elsa: misunderstood, isolated, and confused. That I gained superpowers and had my imaginary friend, Olaf the Snowman, acting as my sense of humor. We could have conjured up a different reality, "holding onto our dreams while letting off steam," all while singing "Let It Go" in our makeshift winter wonderland. Olaf would have liked my warm hugs, despite them being icy and mushy.

Although my dreams had just been shattered and *Frozen* had not even been released yet when I had breastsicles, I did have sleds-ful of love and support during those difficult times from the real characters in my life: my friends and family. They rallied around, coming to visit, preparing meals, and helping with Bob, who was truly our little miracle now that I had miscarried nine times and lost Eliza. They attended the memorial service in below-freezing weather and invited us out to do things even though I, in particular, was not sociable at all. They gave us cards, books, and words of encouragement.

What superpowers can you pull from? Who are your breast buddies to keep you laughing in tough times?

Cabbage Patch Kiddie Breasts

When my CPKBs recovered back to their alluring original form, they made friends with the cabbage that had invaded their space—especially because it had gotten the job done.

Next time I'll just call Brad Pitt.

10

JOAN O FART

Stik-y Business

"Goddamn!" he cried out with glee as he jumped up and down on the couch.

"What did you say?" I inquired slowly, feeling my jaw Slinky to the floor, my ears steam up like Hot Pockets, and my stomach perform a full-twisting tsukahara before saluting the judges.

"Goddamn," he happily repeated for my slack-jawed benefit, soaring so high that his Chapstick fell out of his underwear.

"Cussing is unacceptable!" I boomed authoritatively.

"What's the problem?" he asked. "God is good and a dam holds water!" He smiled at me with the confidence of a thirty-two-year-old football player who has just won the Super Bowl and is "going to Disneyland!"

The problem was that this was my four-year-old, Bob, educating me on vocab structure and definitions. Wearing nothing but his favorite Spiderman briefs, he grabbed his Chapstick, stuck it back into the front slot, and said, "Geez, Mom." Not only had he outsmarted me once again, he had found a dual purpose for the opening in his tighty-whitie–style undies.

On a roll, at the McDonald's drive-through, Bob yelled at the truck in front of us: "Move your f***ing car!" Apparently, this guy was taking too long to pick up his order. Bob wanted his Happy Meal.

In response to this outburst, I shouted: "…!" Nothing. Absolutely nothing. I repeated my internal mantra: *Just ignore it, just ignore it, don't encourage him… Don't encourage him? Wait— Is it too late to return him? Is it too late to return him?*

Anna learned the F-word at age two when Grandma was expressing her dislike for one of the play calls of the Denver Broncos.

Sitting at the dinner table with friends, their preschooler, James, turned to his brother Zach and called him a "poopy head." I held my breath as his dad looked away and controlled any reaction to avoid encouraging James toward further potty mouth.

James tried again: "I like your butt, butt, butt, butt, butt."

Zach, wise beyond his seven years, informed us, "This is a phase he is going through. It is best to ignore him. I read it in a magazine."

What's in a (Business) Name?

You're probably wondering how potty mouth, the whimsical thinking of children, and bodily functions came to play a major role in different aspects of my business, ItStiks. So am I.

My business name may be a snapshot of the childlike innocence with which I used to enjoy shocking those around me—much like Bob, Anna, and James. Some would say I still like to drop bombshells.

Raunchy and rude is a brand image for comedians like Amy Schumer and Rodney Dangerfield. For me as a children's book author, illustrator, and motivational speaker…not so much. I have to MANEtain a sense of professionalism. I must control how greasy my hair gets and how dirty my image is.

One occupational hazard of being a small-business owner, mother, wife, and caregiver is that you have to be a Joan-of-all-trades. Naming my business took copious amounts of time, energy, and brain power—three things that, at my age, come in limited supply. So being low on resources, I had to get creative.

First, I gathered a focus group to brainstorm business name ideas: my kids.

Then I threw a kegger to get people's vote on them. I think my first mistake was serving Mexican food. I made the economical choice of buying beans…a lot of beans. The combination was deadly in more ways than one.

Finally, I referenced the Internet (tool number 2 from my MANEtain Toolbox) and came up with a list of names and slogans to avoid:

"The Most Inappropriate Business Names of All Time"

The Huffington Post, July 30, 2015

PMS Firearms, etc. (rifles, guns, ammo)
Doggie Styles (hot dog stand)
Raper Shop (clothing store)
Moist Realtors
S.T.D. Wines and Liquors
A-Dong Vietnamese restaurant
Stoner Drug (drug store)
Cubic Hair
I got my crabs from Dirty Dick's Crab House
Fochtman Auto Parts
Suck Bang Blow Restaurant & Saloon
Hung Far Low Restaurant

I'VE NEVER MADE A MISTAKE...

Won Kok Restaurant
S & M Mini Mall "Our Dad's Dream Lives On"
Poison Bakery
Sandy Balls (golf course)
T. A. Auto Parts and Services
Hammered Liquor Store
Mr. Cock Babies & Kids
Milkme Idea in a Cup
Fuku Sushi
Anal Teck
Kum & Go
Dumploads on Us (junk removal specialist)

    After all this, I created a business title and an email address that—it turns out—could land on the list above. I wish I could say my children and drunk friends created them, but I made up the parts about the focus group and the kegger. I created my potty-mouth business monickers all on my own.

    ItStiks with you…in your heart, mind, and soul: whimsical presentations and products with a purpose.

    So wonderful, so heartwarming, but… People think I'm saying "It Stinks." What whimsical products and presentations would you imagine me selling? Fart machines? (I do own one of those; see Chapter 21: Laugh of the Day.) Barf in a box? A scoop of cat poop? My presentations could be "Musty and Damp: How to Not Smell Like a Tramp," or "Reach Your Peak Through the Way You Reek," or maybe "Taking Your Fart to Heart."

    While on the topic of bad gas, my email address is JoanOfArt@joanarent.com. My witty title, "Joan of Art," cleverly celebrates the artist in me and markets my art products. Innocent enough, right? Wrong. Read it incorrectly, and it becomes Joan O Fart. Better yet, the full address JoanOFart@JoanARent.com advertises that I am for rent. I am not sure if I am renting my farts or other body parts.

Let's move on to my book *Slumps, Bumps, and Triumphs*. I often refer to it by its initials, SBT, which is misunderstood as SBD: Silent But Deadly. At least its predecessor *Bedtime Is for the Birds* isn't called *Go The F to Sleep*—though I might have titled it that if the name hadn't already been taken.

Luckily, my interactive *Peek-A-Boo Who?* is not mistaken for *Peek-A-Boo Whore*. It's "reveal" pages would surely be quite shocking. My latest work, *Bye, Bye, Booger Bug: The Art of Nose-Picking*, fits the theme perfectly. I figure, why fight the trend?

I didn't see the problems with my wording until it was too late. I often ask myself, *What's a nice girl like me doing, owning a business people call "It Stinks" that has people emailing me at "Joan O Fart"?* I think I gravitate to a twisted perspective. It's hidden in the depths of my reality, and somehow I'm usually the one crossing that line. I admit it's much more fun on the other side.

Cuss Is a Four-Letter-Word

Middleborough, Massachusetts, levies a twenty-dollar fine for swearing in public. If I imposed that rule in my house, I would be

I'VE NEVER MADE A MISTAKE...

richer than Snoop Dogg. Hey—maybe Middleborough should charge *him*. They would make a fortune. But how do you impose civic virtue on a three-year-old? How would I collect? I am sure Snoop would find a way. Heck, I should have found a way...I've realized since learning what my children did during their rebellious, testing-the-boundary-stages of life.

I do believe that my business, with its funny phrases and all it has to offer, embraces the innocence of a child. Consider how words have different meanings for different people.

At my daughter's fifth birthday party, Anna filled up her own goodie bags with lollipops she thought her friends would like. I was not part of the process.

"What does suck mean?" Anna's friend Andrew asked as he unwrapped a sucker from his party bag. Its wrapper said *50 Sucks*.

"That means you get to lick your sucker fifty times," I jumped in, redirecting them from the meaning of "suck" in this context, which would not be good for a child to repeat. "Let's count: 1, 2, 3, 4,...49, 50!" I demonstrated licking the sucker over and over.

"Mrs. and Mr. Gobbermouth..." I addressed Andrew's parents and other concerned parties, rubbing my hands together nervously, shoulders up to my ears, cringing. "The suckers were hand-me-downs from Aunt Edna's fiftieth birthday party," I explained. "I had no idea they were in that box of party decorations!"

Perceiving life with a certain naïveté enhances the ability to feel less pain and live with less fear. Children stumble through life with a gullibility that celebrates joy and laughter. Adopting their budding sense of humor would serve all adults well. It is a refreshing way to bring simplicity to the complexities of life.

Joan O Fart

Fifty sucks, fifty licks, Joan O Fart, Joan of Art... I am not sure how Middleborough, Massachusetts, defines a cuss word. In my house, I could just say any four-letter word is fineable by twenty bucks. I couldn't make money off cussing fees anyway, because I am the master curser. Instead, I am going to continue to capitalize on the *It Stinks, Joan O Fart,* and *SBDs* of my business. I think the brand might just *stink*—ha! I mean *stik*.

11

WHINY-THE-POO

And Triggers Too

Relationships are a crap shoot. When the emotions are a-rockin', the doo-doo comes a-knockin'.

First off, we bring our own poo to the pot, which makes it hard to wade through the crap-ton of feelings that flood our realities. This keeps us stuck in the muck and floating with the Lincoln logs of life.

But it takes two to tango in the day-to-day crapper. Add in siblings and spouses, family and friends, and—*Abra-crap-dabra!*—we are bombarded with others' toilet Twinkies as well, leaving us up the crack without a paddle. Avoiding creamy bohemians can be challenging, to say the least.

We each have our own particular colon cobras that bump up against our butt cheeks. Some suppress our reasoning, while others give rectal feedback that creates splashers. This onslaught makes it difficult to cope, even in the best of times.

Therefore, we can't always see what mother "load" we're dropping into the stress of a situation. Others may deem us "full of shit" because we see only from our own viewpoint.

Hiny Hiders

In hiny-sight, I've learned so many things my siblings and I could have done differently while caring for our mom and Lisa Jean. If only we'd each had the ability to look past our Hiny Hiders* and step out of the stalls boxing us into our own view of things, we could have been more successful at managing the shit-shack of emotions we faced. (*Next time you're in a public restroom, check if the stalls are called Hiny Hiders—it's a thing!)

Taking care of someone who is terminally ill is a hard, hard task. Fertilizer hits the fan. And because of our own hazardous cargo, we drop a wad into the porcelain god known as a *shit*uation.

If Family Weren't Your Family, Would They Still Be Your Friends?

Imagine getting onto a boat with famed *Friends* Chandler, Monica, Ross, Rachel, Joey, and Phoebe for an episode entitled "The One Where Phoebe Is Dying." Now imagine that they aren't friends, but a family who is caring for Phoebe on her deathbed.

Remember: This voyage is one of rough waters in uncharted seas. How would they manage the baggage they each brought to this shituation?

All play dominant roles in the family, so there would be plenty of clashes and anger. Their communication skills aren't great, and oftentimes their personal bias or quirkiness alienates one from the other.

Let's analyze:

- Monica, with her obsessive-compulsiveness, would want to help. However, having to bathe her friend would tip her over the edge, as would her lack of control over Phoebe's failure to get better.

- Chandler would use his sense of humor to deflect his emotions and would be a wimp when it came to making tough decisions, like whether it was time to put Phoebe into hospice.

- Joey would appear clueless, showering Phoebe with love through *doing:* fixing the leaky sink, tacking down the carpet that's tripping him up in the house he grew up in—all the while asking: "How *you* doin'?"

- Rachel would be warm-hearted, making mistakes along the way; she'd communicate by not communicating but would do it all with courage.

- Ross would approach the predicament intellectually, trying to grasp the science behind the slow slipping-away of his loved one. As he painfully grasped at straws for answers that would never come, he would communicate his frustration in the form of dense emotion.

- Phoebe, on her deathbed, would be good-natured and assertive. She might fail to finish her sentences just to be sarcastic in times of stress. She would try to sneak in marijuana-smoking to control her pain.

Other than the pot premise, I can honestly say that I've emulated each of these characters' behaviors at various times.

The episode would end sadly with the loss of Phoebe, but everyone else would have grown closer, having learned that life is full of shitty scenarios and that everyone tries to do their best with who they are and what they bring to a shituaiton.

I'VE NEVER MADE A MISTAKE...

Whiney-the-Poo and Tigger's Triggers

During any given hardship, heed these lessons from Whiny-the-Poo and Toilet-Twinkie Tigger:

- Avoid being Whiny-the-Poo. Whiny-the-Poo can't see the forest from the pee. Whiny wallows in his own poo-pot, and I'm not talking about a honey jar.

- Getting hooked by other Whiny-the-Poos' poo is non-productive, too.

- Beware of Tigger's triggers. Being the primary caregiver does not mean you get to be The Only One making decisions. Conversely, respect that the person who *is* "there"—in the area and/or the home—doing all the bouncy, trouncy, flouncy, pouncy, not-so-fun-fun-fun-fun-fun stuff gets to star in the episode.

- Be like Queen Grimhilde, using the "Mirror, Mirror, on the Wall" to communicate: Encourage people to repeat back what they heard the other person say.

- Be willing to agree to disagree.

- Use "I" statements instead of "you" statements.

- See the positive in each character you interact with and forgive them their flaws. After all, you wouldn't be pissed off at Whiny-the-Poo for his hazardous cargo—he's just too cute and naïve to hold a grudge against. How can you be mad at a bear who says: "You don't spell love, you feel it"? Pooh.

- Apologies help, too.

Siri-ous Miscommunications

Communication is the royal "flush" of success.

Always imagine you're talking to Siri. No matter how clear and crisp and loud you speak, Siri will not always correctly interpret what you said.

I once dictated a text to a caregiver of Lisa Jean's. "Did you read me?" I asked. What she got was: *Did you breed me?* As we are both past breeding age and she is a lesbian, we had to pick up the phone and mirror back what we meant to be communicating. Snaughling was a large part of that phone call.

Communication can be challenging, but done right, it can neutralize the stench of misinterpretation and keep the butt trumpets from blowing it.

Life throws crap at us in many ways, be it a dying parent, financial woes, or a tough relationship. And no matter how hard we try to keep a shituation clean, excretion sneaks through the cracks. To avoid lavatory lockdowns, remember that if you can't trap a crap, you *can* manage its movements. Big movements come in small adjustments.

Manage the BMs—don't let them manage you.

12

CRIMES AGAINST MY SANITY

The Answers Are in How You Play Your Cards

Wanna play a game that asks "What would Grandma find disturbing yet oddly charming?" and gives you the options of "Jell-O," "preteens," or "mouth herpes"?

This is the basis of Cards Against Humanity.

Here are the basic rules:

Each player draws ten white cards.

The person who most recently pooped begins as the Card Czar. (Yes, seriously.) The Card Czar draws a black card and reads the question or fill-in-the-blank phrase out loud to the group.

For example:

What don't you want to find in your Kung Pao Chicken?

What is Batman's guilty pleasure?

I don't need luck! I have _____.

I'VE NEVER MADE A MISTAKE...

The other players answer the question or fill in the blank by selecting a white card from their hand and passing it, facedown, to the Card Czar.

The Card Czar reads the responses aloud, which might be:

Hormone injections

Puppies!

Crystal meth

Full frontal nudity

The Card Czar then picks the funniest solution and whoever submitted it gets one Awesome Point. The player with the most Awesome Points at the end wins.

I have applied this same concept to my own game: Crimes Against My Sanity. The crimes, or black cards, are the happenings of my day. The white cards contain how I can choose to respond to what life has dealt me—ways to manage how the event plays out. I get to choose which white card is the right fix.

I play these black and white cards all day. I don't have much control over the black cards, the events, but I do get to choose how I respond.

Today a black card appeared. It read:

A credit union teller spends 30 minutes giving you incorrect advice on closing your recently deceased mother's account. You then have to spend another 47 minutes correcting the mistake. In response, you_____.

A. Snort Cocaine, run naked through a strawberry field, and scream, "Hey diddle, diddle, I have to piddle."

B. Ask the bank boss to educate the teller by explaining the incorrect information that was provided and then invite them all to dinner with yourself and the Dalai Lama to celebrate everyone's newfound understanding of life.

C. Jump up and down on one leg yelling, "If life's a bowl of cherries, what am I doing in the pits?" while suggesting everyone read the book of the same name by Erma Bombeck.

I chose B, so that the next time someone has this problem, their time will not be wasted like mine. I am still waiting on the Dalai Lama's positive RSVP to our feast.

I wanted to do B *and* C, but I figured C was not a Zen way to manage my stress nor was it worth adding to the teller's burdens, guessing that (a) he had triplets at home from three different women, (b) he was now expecting quadruplets, (c) he was not paid much, and (d) he probably had to deal with a lot of angry people in his job.

A Bull and a Bitch—Which Is Which?

The next black card that upset my sanity asked:

What would you do if you were charged by a red bull, commandeered by a petrified bottle-blonde. (And by red bull, I don't mean the drink—though I think the rider had downed one too many of those.)

I'VE NEVER MADE A MISTAKE...

The options were:

A. Ignore the red bull and its rider, acknowledging that most likely the blonde's brain had fossilized and the reasoning cells were a mere pile of dust in the hollows of her cranium.

B. Face the bull head-on like a matador. Slap the wild beast on the butt, ask "Was that really necessary?", and prance away doing the victory dance!!!!

C. Waggle your fingers at her, singing: "One, two, you're a loose screw. Three, four, you mighty whore. Five, six, you'll regret this. Nine, ten, just try it again!"

D. Toolbox tool 12: Let it go.

In the parking lot of a Walmart in Skowhegan, Maine, I was charged by this bull. The bovine started out parked in an isolated slot, surrounded by nothing but space. As I walked by, about eight feet in front of the monster, I pulled out my phone to check in with my daughter. The bull rider saw me and charged, or rather blared her horn, as though I were blocking her departure. She could have backed up, she could have gone around me, but she chose to blast her warning with her big red Buick, threatening to take me down. I jumped at least three feet in the air while my flip-flops stayed rooted to the asphalt. My shorts and shirt sagged off limbs as they rattled and shook from startlement. The rodeo renegade called me a "bitch" (though not in the same loving terms as my ladies in Uganda) as she roared past me. Now *that* was a Crime Against My Sanity.

Guess which white card I chose?

When challenging a matador, one does what one must do. I slapped the car on the butt and asked the lady, "Was that really necessary?" I did not choose a passive response to the black card. I did what seemed logical at the time. In hindsight, maybe it wasn't the smartest selection, but you know how it is. I won the hand—at least in my mind.

Playing to Win

Life is all about Crimes Against Your Sanity. And you get to choose what is a crime and what makes you insane.

I use death as a barometer: I measure my stressors against the losses I've suffered. If I can survive losing a child, I reason, I can get through anything. That helps me let go of a lot of smaller stuff.

Life is very much like a card game: You choose what cards to play, when to don a poker face, and when to fold.

I get to protect my mind against events that encourage me to lose it. I get to win at my game of life: Crimes Against My Sanity.

13

MY COUNTRY—
RIGHT OR WRONG?

A Lottery With No Winners

"MY COUNTRY-FREE OR NOT!" was the theme of an essay which won special honors for Joan ▮▮▮▮▮▮▮▮. Keith Vaughan of the Columbine Sertoma Club presented Joan a very special plaque and a radio at an awards assembly Feb. 28.

**My Country—
Free or Not!**
by Joan Arent
Sertoma Essay Winner

A family sits and watches TV for only one reason. The most interested is a young man of eighteen. If the announcer on the screen calls his number, he won't be watching TV for a very long time.

Silence fills the room. His mother thinks she hears her son's number. The announcer calls out: "2-9-5-7." The father and mother start praying. The youngest who doesn't understand lets out a giggle.

The young man stands up but doesn't say a word; he just stands there thinking. He is not afraid to fight if he must, but he does not like the idea of killing and destroying.

Soon he is waving from a window of an army plane. There are tears, but everyone knows he must go.

On the way to camp, men start talking to each other. One asks the eighteen-year-old why he came; he had a choice.

"Sure I have a choice," he agrees sarcastically. "Either I go to war or sit in a dirty jail somewhere. You call that a choice?"

The young man went into combat with his friends against the enemy. Their days and nights were filled with the whistles of bullets and bombs exploding. In March, news came that President Nixon was going to start releasing soldiers in May. Some were excited, but this man wasn't—he had heard those words before. Still, he prayed he would be getting out of this hell. Days passed, and his unit moved closer to Saigon. On Friday, April 16, 1971, the man who was once a boy died by walking over a booby trap.

Before he died, this free man wrote this poem:

My Country, Right or Wrong
When a child is born, his mind is clean.
The hate, the war, the violence
cannot be foreseen.
His life is shaped by the world around him,
and soon the burden is pushed upon him.
He leaves to fight and shoot and kill,
and all this of his own free will.
War is a great and mighty thing,
of which there are many songs to sing.
People cry, "My country, right or wrong.
Let's go destroy the Viet Cong."
They give a man a gun
and say he is a soldier,
and tell him, with this gun,
to kill a fellow soldier.
On each side, there are men
who think they are right,
and each believes it is his freedom
for which they fight.
They care little about the shape of a table,
but shall fight for their country
as long as they are able.
While their leaders question over who
shall enter through which door,
the soldiers wonder who
the waiting coffins are for.
Their guns are aimed
at the head of the enemy,

and they wonder why
they play God to so many.
They live in a world of strife,
of life and death,
and wonder why
they have the power to bring death.

This free man was my brother. My country—free or not?

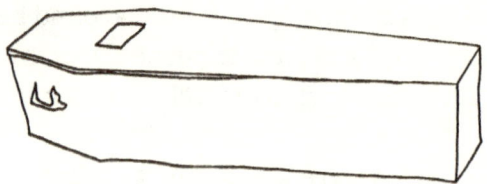

Death-Dodging

It has been forty-five years since my brother Matt died in Vietnam. I was eleven years old and in the sixth grade. The pain of his loss has lessened, but the sorrow sleeps deep within my heart, awakened from its slumber when I revisit his poem and the essay I won honors for in a contest at St. Therese Catholic School.

Matt wrote his poem while in Vietnam. He mailed it to our mom and dad months before he died. Imagine how helpless they must have felt, receiving his poem and having no power to come to the aid of their second oldest child.

The loss of Matt ripped at my heart, leaving it bruised and battered. To this day, it stops beating whenever someone dies.

As the third youngest of eight, I was hurting but not old enough to understand why there was a war and how to handle my despair. My parents and siblings did their best to help me while managing their own grief.

I was impotent in a world that seemed so unjust. Why would one of my protectors depart to an unreachable place? How could I extinguish that ache of wanting to say, "Hi, Big Brother. When are you coming home?" That yearning to walk with my small hand tucked into the warmth and security of his? What person had the will to plant a land mine that silenced the heartbeat of one so dear to me and left my own heartbeat barely a whisper?

Death is a mystery. Matt's passing was my first life tutorial. I created my own warzone. My defense was to shut down my heart to protect myself from any more loss, suffering, and confusion. Life couldn't be trusted. I was ready to fight.

Some who have never experienced death, live as if it will never happen. I lived as if waiting for its arrival. I played hide-and-seek with love and death until death found me again, and again. Only when my daughter Eliza died twenty-three years later did I stop fearing loss of life; surrendering to the inevitable was less exhausting than preoccupying my mind with the what-ifs, which served only to create a fury that could not be calmed.

I do not fear my own death. Death no longer vanquishes me; it reminds me to celebrate each breath.

A Home in My Heart

When a child is born, his mind is clean.
The hate, the war, the violence cannot be foreseen.
His life is shaped by the world around him,
and soon the burden is pushed upon him.

As so tragically expressed in Matt's poem, the burden of Matt's death was pushed upon my mind so clean. The loss of him and of others has shaped my world up through this day. I am forever steeled for someone I love to be snatched from me. Ever-aware that death

I'VE NEVER MADE A MISTAKE...

sits on the sidelines, ready to take control of the game. I am part of the crowd, with no power over the outcome—only dominance over how I respond.

I did not want to be alone with the agony that moved into my soul at age eleven and built its walls and structures. But this construction process and the nails hammered in by my losses provided a foundation for my compassion.

Eliza's death was another lesson that added brick and mortar to my edifice of understanding life and death. In suffering that loss, I walked through the doors that had closed when Matt died. They reopened as I learned that I was not alone and that I could recover—and not only could, but should.

I finally learned that the home built in my heart by my pain could also house happiness and healing.

14

DO YOU HAVE GAS?

Set Your Boundaries

I have GAS. It follows me everywhere. This churning, invisible, odorless, relentless, gripping condition. It doesn't matter if I limit my dairy, increase my lactose, or suck on a whale's tail. It doesn't help if I stand on my head or do the hokey-pokey. I am sure I burst forth from the womb glowing with GAS. Maybe it's because I'm a Libra. Or because I lied to a priest at Confession: "Bless me, Father, for I have sinned; I made a toad do a back-flip in a petticoat."

I know others who have GAS—some just a little, others a lot. I see it in women more than men, teachers more than CEOs. It can rear its uninvited head (or, shall I say, backend) in the most undesirable places. As I age, it is more pronounced.

Early GAS Detection

My son sticks his head into the living room. "You are a danger to yourself," he warns.

"What do you mean?" I respond. "Is it because my SIM card stopped simmering? Did I tweet the wrong thing on Facebook? Did I Instagram the ham too long?"

"I'm talking about what you're doing to your atmosphere," he groans. "Your condition is creating a buildup of pressure that could damage your ozone layer."

"Is that worse than when I put hair gel under my armpits and deodorant in my hair?"

"It's only going to cause you pain," he urges. "I can see the distension."

"If I belch, will that help?"

"Eructation is not enough. You have to manage this," he says. "Otherwise you're going to blow a raspberry."

"I did that at church once, sitting on a wooden pew," I muse. "It wasn't pretty."

"Mother, you've *got* to take this seriously," my son pleads. "I mean, you are going to come down with some horrible disease like hoof-in-mouth if you don't take control."

"Start by kicking Fabio out of your bed," my daughter chimes in. "He's wearing you down. And stop doing my dishes if I leave them in the sink."

"Stop leaving them in the sink," I protest.

"Stop bloating."

"I think you mean gloating."

"You get gassed up too easily," explains my son. "Maybe you should try surrounding yourself with others who have GAS—start a support group. Give Oprah a call. She'll help you out."

"Good idea!" I say. "I'll bake cookies for the meeting. I'll make a peanut butter batch for the gluten-free-sucks-to-be-me attendees, chocolate-chip for the peanut-allergic, brownies for those who don't like cookies, and cabbage cranberry soup for those who think every day is Passover."

"Mom—you've got to chillax!" cries my daughter. "Do something for yourself!!"

"How do I do that?" I ask.

The Smell of GAS

GAS is the I GIVE A SHIT disease. It can be a blessing and a curse. It's a great way to make friends...even those you don't want. If it turns into diarrhea, you're in trouble.

Who has GAS? Look around. Is it your neighbor who goes out of his way to make sure he shares his prize-winning eight-foot zucchini from his garden with you? Or maybe it's the woman bagging your groceries who takes extra care that the frozen food is not with the perishables and that the baggage space is maximized.

Just doing their job, you might think.

Well, stop and take notice: If your bagger plants your gallon-size bottle of Pleasant-Scent Fabuloso on top of your bacon-flavored toothpaste and then throws a twenty-pound bag of Miracle Mulch onto the bouquet you're buying for your friend whose perverted neighbor died when the drone he sent to "stream" her in the shower boomeranged back into his temple at thirty miles per hour as he sat naked in his hot tub…then there is a bagger who *doesn't* have GAS.

But GAS can work against you. This disease hit my friend, a Special Education teacher named Maddie, hard.

Monday through Friday she is up at 4:30 a.m. peeling grapes, deseeding mandarins, and taking the pom out of the pomegranates for her kids' lunches. Darning socks, spit-polishing shoes, steam-ironing underwear, shining the gerbil's nails—this is all before she throws in two loads of laundry.

"Who wants eggs for breakfast?" she asks.

"I'll have eggs without the eggs."

"I want hash browns with extra hash."

"I want Fruit of the Loom Fruit Loops."

"Mom, I'm a Paleo-lunan, you know! I only eat meat, dairy, and eggs during high tide and I don't eat veggies at low tide."

"Here's a bowl of Tide," offers Maddie. "You figure it out. If you add water, it'll eliminate the need for you to brush your teeth: soap, suds, and breakfast all in one."

Finally—after canning peaches and filling twenty-nine scrapbook pages, creating a memory lane for each of her ten children in book form to be passed on from generation to generation to celebrate the highlights of the boys' and girls' lives, combining to equal four hundred eighty-two pages (and that's just for a single year)—Maddie leaves the house for work by 6:30 a.m.

She comes home at 6:00 p.m., makes rump roast without the rump (because eating rump would be *grooooossss*"), starts the dirty-dozen homework march, folds the laundry, and dynamites dust bunnies.

"Honey, are my clothes ready for my meeting tomorrow?" asks her husband. "Honey, why are you drinking that whole bottle of cough syrup and tying that 'Jesus Loves You' shoestring around your neck? Hey, while you're on the toilet, could you clean it?"

After she is done dying, Maddie must create a lesson plan for Junior, who is one of her special needs students who needs extra-special attention because his parents who don't have GAS forgot to pick him up from school because they were out drinking at a bar at 3:00 p.m.

Who else has GAS? The caregivers who take care of your mom with Alzheimer's and your sister with cancer, all for such low wages that they have to work three jobs to pay the bills. Those are the ones who have GAS.

Who doesn't have GAS in your life? The guy who deliberately cuts you off while you're getting in the elevator, pushes the button for his floor, and doesn't hold the door as you're trying to get on with your two broken legs in casts with your crutches about to cross the threshold. Who doesn't have GAS? The woman who yells at the ticket agent because the plane is late and she's going to miss seeing her poodle that has a wardrobe larger than Miley Cyrus's. Who doesn't have GAS? Donald Trump…oh, never mind—it comes out of his mouth.

Manage Your GAS Flow

So GAS is not all bad. It teaches you compassion and empathy. It attracts good people who help you through hard situations. It teaches you how to survive and thrive in difficult times. GAS can bring you great joy—a feeling of purpose and being needed. You can be part of changing the world. Martin Luther King Jr., Maya Angelou, Malala Yousafzai, Mother Teresa, Tawakkol Karmn, and Liu Xiaobo all have or had GAS.

Having GAS has taught me to give to those who give back—to focus on the rewards of GAS. People will give to you because you have GAS. They will hold you up when you are down. You will do the same for them. They will be there for you in times of need, especially when they see you sinking due to your GAS affliction.

How do you prevent GAS from over-accumulating and becoming overbearing? You set boundaries. Say yes to yourself and no to others. Give to yourself. Communicate with others. Surround yourself with other GAS-sy people. D.O.T., D.O.T., D.O.T. Don't Over Think. Write it down in pen and ink. Do a D.O.T. dump and let it out!! Don't over ANALyze. Stand up for yourself; don't be somebody's rug or app-wipe.

Do you have GAS? Most of us do—and we should. We just need to manage the bad and the good.

ANALyze your GAS. It'll be a blast!!!!!!

15
THE ART OF MANEtainance

The Affordable Hair Act in Action

When life gets hairy, I aim for an aura that speaks calm, cool, and collected. Although I may be splitting hairs behind the scenes, outwardly I rock the message: *All is tamed. There is nothing I can't untangle.*

I put time and money into my clothes, my nails, my makeup, and my locks. My hair is the crown jewel to the package, reminding me that I am *not* having a bad hair day. Or, if I am, I can manage. When my tresses are in control, I am in control…or am I?

As you know, hair has a mind of its own. It grows in random locations with little purpose: up, down, bouncy, bold, limp, lackluster—a summary of life in one bouffant hairdo gone bad. Hair sprouts as sporadically as it does quickly in areas of no net worth, and at the pace of a slug looking for supper, in others. It won't grow in places it used to and it pops up in spots you never considered.

We think our hair makes a true difference in whether we'll find our purpose for existing, our soul mate, or at least our duck mate. Ducks mate for life.

Hair We Go Again

Like plucked hairs, difficult problems return with a vengeance. Sometimes we have to try various tactics to stop the invasion of the unattractive. We also have to look in the mirror and figure out what *we're* doing that keeps them coming back.

Men like my college-calamity boyfriend Harold popped up in my life like boob hairs. You know the ones: not there one day and the next you could make a donation to Locks of Love.

Like those hairs, the men who latched on to me weren't very appealing. But they continued to grow on me because I didn't know any better.

Hair Today, Gone Tomorrow

One was Kevin, the garbage truck driver. I kinda liked him until he showed up in his trash truck at my house, which I happened to be sharing with my parents and siblings.

Ding-dong! went the doorbell.

"Is Joan home?" Kevin inquired.

"No, she left to borrow sugar from President Reagan," Mom deferred.

"She did not!" my sister Lisa revealed, pointing at me. "She's hiding behind the front door."

Did I mention he had taken me out to dinner at Benihana's the night before? That sounds great, except he had to borrow money from the guy sitting next to us. Thank heavens that guy came prepared with his wallet; I almost went home with *him*.

I used tool number 7: I pulled out my **Gorilla Glue** and set boundaries. I never called Kevin back and did nothing to encourage him. My parents were disappointed: They wanted free trash pickup.

Highlighting the Good

After that, it still took me a long time to learn that I deserved a cut above the rest. That I was light years a*head* of the men I was letting entangle my life.

I finally decided to highlight my attributes and stop being the hair gel wrangling the strays.

I used tool 11: **Brush and Blow.** After washing away grease like Kevin, I redirected my life the way I wanted it to head by being pickier about whom I gave my parents' number and address to.

I made a list of requirements for the new men in my life. They had to:

a. Drive a real car.
b. Clean their teeth.
c. Own a wallet with money and a credit card in it.

I sought out men who were head and shoulders above the unruly other pluckers I had been letting into my life.

Glug, Cluck, and Pluck

This world has all types of hairs—and people—that we must learn to deal with.

For example, I used to think *my* chin was the only one on Earth that sported shocks of dark hair like the sword in the stone: sharp, stiff, and stuck. My face is smooth as a baby's bottom one minute, and then *rip, slice*...the hand snags on that one hair that wouldn't let all the king's horses and all the king's men by. I could hang my pearls and my laundry out to dry on that hair. I call these my "chin-hair hangers." They are hard, erect, and ready to perform.

Now that I know others have these hairs, I am going to start a new trend: People will be walking around town with their sunglasses and jewelry dangling from their chins.

But at first, I thought only old people were plagued by unwanted facial hair. I was wrong: My twenty-six-year-old niece and her bosom buddies have wine, cheese, and hair-plucking parties. But maybe the younger generation's "problem strands" are like blades of grass in the wrong place: soft, supple, and lacking the capacity to serve as a beer stand. Still, I think I've been missing out. These get-togethers sound more fun and far more practical than those Cocktails and Canvas parties.

So come on over to my place for a glug, cluck, and pluck party—I'll supply the hairs! You can even rest your beer on my chin-hair hanger.

MANEtain Your Relationships

Changing your life can be like maintaining your hair. Some growth is slow and tedious, and changes must be made one pluck at a time. You can untangle the knots or you can chop 'em.

Learn from your experiences. Log them in your mind and in your heart so you don't repeat them.

Think how you can embrace and expand the Affordable Hair Act. Pull out that MANEtain Toolbox and try different tools at different times with different problems.

For example, if you have a friend who seems more like a frenemy but bold cuts aren't your style, invite her to your glug, cluck, and pluck party and try tool number 3: Share your feelings with her to see if you can straighten her out. If that doesn't curl her mane into action, then pluck her. Life is full of sacrifices.

If you have friends who are cliquish and treat you poorly, use tool 9 in your resource box: Wax them away all at once.

If you work with a difficult boss, use tools 1, 3, 4, and 7. You decide the order:

1. **Magnifying Mirror:** Sometimes you aren't able to change the other person or the dilemma. So look in the mirror and see what *you* can change.

3. **Hairdresser:** Verbalize your perspective and needs; compile a list of potential remedies.

4. **Battle Plan:** Decide how you are going to handle the situation.

7. **Gorilla Glue:** Set your boundaries; decide which behaviors you are willing to deal with.

Use your AHA moments—you know: your Affordable Hair Act experiences—to practice the tools in your MANEtain Toolbox and improve your life.

Try Knot to Worry

Find the least energy-draining way to solve your problems. When things feel like a completely tangled mess, do nothing. Let your hair go, stress less, and give the situation time to work out. Life, like your hair, is manageable if you don't care so much.

So simply wash away the dirt, blow-dry in the direction you want things to go, shave a shock of hair into submission, and have fun with what you can't control.

Go for bold and bouncy, not limp and lackluster. Well-sprung can have its benefits—and not just for a penis.

16

A FORTY-YEAR-OLD VIRGIN

STDs Without the Fun

Uncharted, unexplored—that's what my life had come to. I am not sure why it took me so long to enjoy the pleasures of this particular experience. What had I been missing out on all these years? Forty years old I was, and living without it. Maybe I should have joined a support group for late-bloomers.

To add insult to injury, STDs were driving my celibacy. STDs are hard to live with, especially when you're a virgin. Where's the fun in that?

STDs made me do lousy on tests. I didn't get jobs because I bombed interviews. They kept me from moving ahead in my career; I was a professional speaker who was afraid of crowds. My social life suffered. I mean, how do you meet guys with that kind of secret?

I was immobilized, unable to make decisions. I let people take advantage of me. When a teacher in high school looked down my shirt, my STDs kept me from reporting him. When a professor in college crossed the line, my STDs told me it was my fault. Communication with my husband was strained because my STDs made me defensive. I lacked assertiveness as a parent, which encouraged my children to verbally spank me.

Withering Erotica

I was naïve to the pleasures I could have enjoyed if I just gave in, didn't fight so hard. But with all the outside influences, how was I to know? In fact, I blame Fabio for some of this. He contributed to my STDs by coming where he wasn't wanted. He led my mind masturbations in the wrong direction.

Fabio told me that losing my virginity was overrated. That I could do without. But I knew he was wrong. I knew staying a virgin meant he could control me. That having any type of STD was what kept him in my bed at night. And that if I lost my virginity, I could decrease his effectiveness in the sack by sixty percent. I would have self-confidence. I would move forward in life, be more successful.

Fighting the Vows of Chastity

So, what are STDs? Self-Traumatizing Doubts.

How did I kick them and lose my virginity? It didn't just happen out of thin air. It took time—and lots of work.

First off, I accepted that my previous strategies hadn't been effective at all.

I'd had boob job after boob job, a facelift, a tummy tuck, Botox, spot removal, eyebrow enhancement, and hair extensions. Who doesn't want to keep trying to be better, do better, and look better, especially with STDs lurking in the shadows?

Okay, so the first boob job was a Victoria Secret Water Bra. You know, the ones with the breast cups filled with water that go *splosh, splish, splash* whenever you throw out your hip or do a Bruce/Caitlyn Jenner discus throw. (I still have trouble deciding which name to reference here. Is he a he when we discuss the discus throw, or is he always a she? I digress.) Water bras made my boobs sound like gum boots sloshing through Hurricane Harvey runoff. That was a problem.

Boob job number two was the Victoria Secret Wonderbra. The problem was that when I wore it, people wondered what watermelon I had merged with.

I used Photoshop to erase wrinkles in promotional headshots as a makeshift facelift, but it did nothing for the Grand Canyon waterways on my actual face. I should have stopped squinting when I was five like my mother told me to.

Botox in my belly was about as sexy as Jack Black in *Nacho Libre*, and the tummy tuck was the thirteen inches of mesh cross-stitched into my stomach—okay, so maybe those two don't count.

The spot removal was foundation, the eyebrow enhancement was a makeup pencil, and the extensions were one of those hairpieces that could have won a Muskrat Love contest.

I even read a book on celibacy—true story. In fact, that is how I met my husband. He spotted me on a beach. We chatted. I stepped on to my windsurfer to sail away. He asked me if we could go out some time. "Are you Brad Pitt?" I asked. When he said, "No, but I *am* a gynecologist; I'm good with my hands," I said, "*Purr*, sure. Please put your number in my bag on the sand."

He slid a scrap of paper with his phone number into the celibacy book and then he asked for mine. Laughingly, I gave it to him, figuring I'd never hear from him again. But it turns out, he didn't have STDs; he knew what he wanted and he went after it. The rest is history.

BDSM: Whipping My Psyche Into Submission

Despite all these desperate measures, I was still slave to my STDs. I knew I had to put into practice my BDSMs and embrace my SEBs. (This is starting to sound like a government report.)

To effectively deal with my Self-Traumatizing Doubts, I first needed to define them. Mine included but were not limited to:

- Harsh inner critic
- Self-intimidation
- Overreactive panic
- Vulnerability
- Fear of failure
- Irrational thinking

I was a virgin to self-confidence. I needed a tougher layer of skin. So I tried various roleplaying to step past my own limitations. I was aggressive. I limited my passive behavior. I took my BDSMs seriously:

B for Bondage: *I bound and gagged my inhibitions. I took risks. I sought out experiences and mentors. I watched others shed their inner-critic chains and quiet the snap of the irrational-thinking whips that kept them immobilized. If others could let go of their innocence, so could I.*

D for Dominance: *I found ways to dominate my self-doubts. I replaced negative thoughts with positive ones.*

S for Submission: *I beat my fears into submission with mental clamps and meditated daily to control my thoughts. Fabio never had a chance. I took note of my accomplishments to reinforce that I would and could succeed, and had nothing to fear.*

M for Sadomasochism: *I embraced the idea that inflicting pain on myself and others was simply a non-pleasurable experience. Plus, I learned to let go by accepting the acronym letter M here, when this word clearly starts with an S. Maybe Fabio can explain it—he seems to be an expert in this area.*

I replaced my STDs with SEBs: Self-Efficacy Beliefs (coined by Bandura):

- Mastery of experience
- Sense of well-being
- Accomplishments
- High aspirations
- Commitment
- Reduced stress
- Kicking Fabio out of my bed—or at least my mind

Finally, after years and years and years of experimentation and experiences, at forty years old I was able to pop my cherry. It was exhilarating!

The Budding of My Lotus

For the first time in my life, I felt sure of myself. I could go to the grocery store and not feel guilty standing in the express line, unsure mathematically if I really had fifteen items or less. (It was the dozen eggs that threw me off. Did their multiplicity exclude me from living large and checking out in the fast lane of life?)

I had gotten past feeling guilty for using the last square of toilet paper at the airport bathroom.

I had evolved from feeling the need to tell all sixteen women in line that there was no toilet paper in stall seven. I restrained from using the white paging telephone to announce the toilet paper deficit.

I celebrated that if I forgot to bring bags into the grocery store, I still had the puffy ones under my eyes. The store even offered five cents for providing my own, so I made money off one of my most disliked facial features!

I found my voice: I yelled encouragement at my daughter's basketball game without worrying about offending anyone.

I stopped turning at every "turn on left arrow" sign. I no longer parked for hours at STOP signs, waiting for permission to go. I even learned to rebel a little. Driving toward the digital solar-powered speed limit sign flashing at me as if to say: "Hey, you—yeah, I mean you!! Do you see what speed you are going?", I shifted my MINI coop into high gear, flipped off the one-legged speed cop with my windshield wipers, and sped up to the suggested speed limit. I felt like Danica Patrick!

I accepted that my fan club was never going to have a Taylor Swift–sized following. I embraced that I would never get three hundred seven million likes for my selfie in my red hot chili pepper lipstick with matching one-piece swimsuit and bunny slippers. Taylor had more zoom in her zoombas, more swish in her sway. My swish was more of a *splash* and *splosh:* the sound of my Victoria's Secret Water Bra.

STD Side Effects

Studies have shown that STDs can keep people from speaking up in meetings, taking on projects at work, and taking risks. STDs can cause us to apologize for the hole in our underwear that no one can see and for the garlic breath no one can smell. We tell our children and husband, "I know you're busy, so it's not important that you come to my choir performance" while thinking, *They should know I want them there.*

Guilt and self-doubt are often intertwined like two Pillsbury Doughboy rolls wrestling for space on an overcrowded baking sheet. Or in a love fest. Visualize two croissants having sex—or not.

Guilt is feeling bad about something. Self-doubt is much more insidious.

Self-doubt is being unsure enough of yourself to contract diarrhea of the mouth in hopes of getting validation for your new haircut, clothing choices, breath mints. You know you have STDs when you explain to the bag checker at the grocery store why you chose a green sweater instead of purple to go with your brown pants. You're seeking fashion approval from a guy wearing a t-shirt that says *Kiss me: I'm a fungi.* Or when you apologize to the cashier for not following Julia Child's suggestion of pairing cordon bleu with wild rice and a shiitake mushroom reduction sauce, knowing full well that the only chef this cashier is probably old enough to know is the Swedish one in the Muppets.

And now, self-doubt can be taken to a whole new level thanks to social media. For example, when you don't get a thumbs up for your Rottweiler-reminiscent hairdo. The rulebook doesn't tell you that with all those people viewing your post, there's no way you are going to get everyone to substantiate your choices.

The Taste of Nectar, Oh So Sweet

I suggest you give up your STDs and lose your virginity, too. You'll move ahead in life a lot quicker!

As a child, you rolled over and then took your first steps, all because you knew you could—or better yet, because nobody told you you couldn't. Eventually voices of doubt crept in and that's when you first contracted STDs. Left untreated, these Self-Traumatizing Doubts continued to fester.

Now that you are grown, try not to let those voices hold you in bondage that keeps you from living your dreams. It's not that you can't question yourself; but consider to what extent you take out that hammer and beat yourself up.

J Bowman, lead guitarist of Michael Franti & Spearhead, says, "Regrets and mistakes are only lessons that haven't been learned."

Finding a way to benefit from your painstaking trials and painful tribulations decreases your learning curve. Think how much further ahead you could be by releasing regret quickly. How much time you could save growing wiser and becoming stronger, more successful.

Use a compass to guide you through your next experience and heed your BDSMs: Use "Bondage" to muzzle your inhibitions; establish "Dominance" over self-doubts; beat your fears into "Submission"; and refrain from mental "Sado(M)asochism."

Look beyond the problem and seek clarity on how to solve it.

And when you do, let that drop of confidence-nectar engulf your tongue. Savor the emotions of triumph.

Drag Queens: Poster Children of SEBs

While traveling in El Salvador, our hotel desk clerk named Pablo was our knight in shining armor.

Every morning, I would ask Pablo to put our passports and other valuables in the hotel's four-by-four-foot metal safe. This safe put the droid BB-8 to shame. It had a mind of its own. It was big and brass, and it was stubborn. Every night Pablo would unlock the safe and out would come the goodies. A couple of times the safe resisted Pablo's advances, but Pablo always prevailed.

At 7:00 p.m. on our last night there, I requested our things out of the safe, since we would be leaving for the airport at 4:00 a.m. I asked for Pablo, but he wasn't working. The two young men on duty struggled, cursed, banged, slammed, and kicked the safe to no avail.

At 10:00 p.m. I desperately suggested that they call Pablo.

After another painstaking sixty minutes, into the dark room walked a beautiful woman with long luxurious locks, a sultry complexion, and a quiet demeanor. My heart sank; where was Pablo? He seemed to be the only one who could tame this beast of a safe. What if we couldn't get our passports out and we couldn't get on the plane? What if we were stranded here forever—or at least one more day?

Not to worry, within minutes she had opened the safe. I rushed to thank her and stopped short with a gasp of delight. It *was* Pablo. The updo, the eyeliner, the peach lip gloss, the double-D breasts, the sway without the slosh…he—she—was like an angel from heaven. That, and the fact that he had my passports in hand.

Now, *that* is embracing your inner beauty and being comfortable with your own Self-Efficacy Beliefs. I think we could all learn a thing or two from cross-dressers.

Seek out your own role models. If they can do it, you can. A waiter with whom my girlfriends and I bonded over the course of two hours of comings and goings set down my Hanky Panky cocktail and confided, "It took me forty years to love myself. I wish it hadn't taken so long."

I'll drink to that.

Find the Key to Your Chastity Belt

It was a challenge to give up the celibacy that had gripped my life like a chastity belt with no key. To release my inner goddess and mind-masturbate myself into a world of self-confidence.

Who cares if my size fifteen goddess feet don't compliment my dance moves like Taylor Swift's? Who cares if my family photo gallery looks like an earthquake rocked just that particular hallway of my house? Who cares that my child is not a star athlete or as a good a student as the helicopter mom's who isn't allowed to live and breathe for himself? Who cares that my daughter marches to her own drum—that she spray-paints her nose hair purple, has a pierced left pinky, and dyes her bangs the color of the flamingos in our front yard? Who cares that my butt resembles two Volkswagen Bugs?

The problem is that at some point, we all do care. Which is why giving up your STDs and virginity is for a good cause: your mental health. Embrace your SEBs and utilize your BDSMs. Don't wait forty years to pop your cherry.

17

LSD, SIT-INS, AND ME

You *Can* Redirect Your Life

Legal advice is always a good thing, especially when LSD is involved. Fortunately I have a good lawyer. I wrote him a letter to update him on what could have made for an episode of *Breaking Bad*. It was one of those many letters that acted as therapy in times of stress. It kept me from eating my young, popping a hallucinogen, or experimenting with any number of other brain-numbing drugs.

I'VE NEVER MADE A MISTAKE...

Mental illness can create demons that make the sufferer feel like they're on LSD, cause bystanders to think they're on LSD, and overall make for complicated situations. My attorney got to act as both my legal and mental counselor.

> Dear Mr. Lawyer,
>
> I wanted you to know of the fun we have all been having. That way, if I end up in jail for cat-daddling or Lisa Jean lands behind bars for impersonating a traffic cone, you'll know where to find us and can hopefully post bail.
>
> My sister decided to hold a sit-in in a parking garage. One can only guess what she was protesting: unfair wages for her attorney (you); unjust treatment of the mice in Cinderella; maybe she simply wanted to redirect traffic. If the latter, she accomplished her goal.
>
> L.J. was accompanied by a government-paid caregiver, and one must have a safety plan in place if one's ward decides to pull a Greensboro-like stand...er, sit, that is. (Who knows if L.J. even knows if a person is black or white?) I do solemnly testify that no LSD was involved—though she was tripping on Ritalin. Clearly, it was not a good high. Not even the caregiver was enjoying it.
>
> The safety plan requires that the person in charge of L.J. be given permission to do the "catch and release" maneuver (similar to noodling or cat-daddling) on their client, whereby should the fish (client) decide to swim away or hide in a hole, the fisherman (caregiver) stands poised to catch the slippery little devil with bare hands. Of course, once the fish is controlled and making good decisions, it will be released.
>
> Now I have to "sit in" myself on two meetings to set up a protocol for my throwback hippie sister who suffers from Down syndrome,

Alzheimer's, and OCD. Who needs drugs when one can have those mind maladies?

I may have to enlist your services for L.J.'s cameo appearance on *Saturday Night Live*. She is going to teach people how to do The Plop. This is when she sits down wherever she wants, whenever she wants—much like a traffic cone. A modern, trendy, turn-heads traffic cone. Follow us on Twitter, Facebook, YouTube, Snapchat, and CDOT (Colorado Department of Transportation). One must always look on the bright side of things: At least she didn't pretend to be a traffic cone on I-70—though she could have proven useful during heavy-weekend ski season.

You should also know that I placed Mom in hospice care today, due to the fact that she is sleeping more, eating less, and walking less. Plus, it's hard for us children to take care of managing her when we are busy plopping down next to Lisa "The Plopper" Jean to protect her.

I don't think Mom could even participate in a sit-in. Woolworth's is happy.

Sincerely,
Mary Dew Furrybush

Funny Farm Fun

Sometimes I just break out singing "They're coming to take me away, ha ha! They're coming to take me away..." I might *not* mind going to the funny farm to see those "nice young men" in their "clean white coats." Napoleon XIV who wrote that song totally understood how I felt.

In order to avoid jail (and bail), the funny farm, and LSD, I had to step back and look at my tools for handling circumstances like these. Using tweezers would have definitely landed me in jail, so tool 6 from the MANEtain Toolbox was not an option. *Can't see it, it ain't a problem*—tool 12—also would not work, because clearly all those cars lined up behind her could see her (thank heavens).

In the end, I used a lot of tools to redirect the problems-slash-traffic and stop the spiraling of the situation. I called in all our resources and took the following steps:

1. We avoided taking Lisa Jean to areas that weren't safe.
2. We got support from experts:
   - Two teachers in a classroom of twenty special needs children assured us: "If we can handle this, you can handle this."
   - They wrote up an intervention plan.
   - They came in weekly to teach us how to help Lisa Jean, my mom, and the caregivers.
3. Hospice helped care for Mom while we found resources for Lisa Jean.

We were all lost; the experts helped us find ourselves.

Springing from the Stalemate

Who is having a sit-in in your life? Your mate, refusing to compromise about a certain situation? Your business partner, wanting full control over the decision-making process?

Consider your options. Call in your resources. Come up with a win-win to reverse the stall. Communicate your needs, change the lenses on your glasses, and determine how to view the stand-off with a sense of humor.

How are you going to redirect your life? Is The Plop your most effective tool, or the most destructive? We know LSD is not the answer, but maybe a little Gorilla Glue. No, not to sniff! Use it to set boundaries.

And try not to worry. Look at the bright side.

Lisa Jean taught us a thing or two, including The Plop, yet she is not a squished traffic cone. She is an amazing young woman who always brings laughter and joy to my life. Plus, she has the power to redirect traffic.

18

THE TORMENTOR

Alzheimer's Sucks

Y ou asked us to come, a gathering of the minds, many of which were slipping away, yours included. Your intention was to bond us together, fight this battle as a team. The problem was there was no game plan. How can there be with a disease as evil as a Dementor, with death as its end goal?

> "Dementors…glory in decay and despair; they drain peace, hope, and happiness out of the air around them…If it can, the Dementor

will feed on you long enough to reduce you to something like itself… soulless and evil. You will be left with nothing but the worst experiences of your life."

—Harry Potter and the Prisoner of Azkaban

My mother had invited all her children to a support group for those in the early stages of a death sentence. This vibrant woman who had skied until age seventy-three was now, at seventy-six, buried in an avalanche of emotions over her diagnosis of Alzheimer's, a terminal illness so devastating it should be called the *Tormentor*.

"Tormentors will suck every good feeling, every happy memory out of you. They can consume a person's soul, rendering their victims but an empty shell. They cannot be destroyed, BUT THEY WILL DESTROY YOU and often the relationships around you."

—Joan Arent, discussing Alzheimer's

The frigidness of this disease would sweep all of us along—Mom's children, her children-in-law, and her grandchildren—through many a fall, winter, spring, and summer. Yet Mom alone lived in a grey, dark world, plunged ever deeper into a chasm of emptiness. Unlike the changing of the seasons, she experienced no budding and blossoming of the brain, no burst of color and hope, no blast of warmth or thawing of her forgetfulness and confusion.

The Tormentor crept into her mind so slowly, it was hard to discern which signs were a natural part of the aging process.

2002: The Tormentor Knocks

"Someone's at the door!" Mom called out.

"I'll get it," my sister-in-law Jane offered.

"No, don't!" Mom cried.

"Why not?" I asked, bewildered. "What's wrong?"

"They're dangerous," Mom warned.

"They aren't dangerous," I assured her. "They're delivering flowers."

"Are you sure?"

"I can see the bouquet," Jane said.

"What if that's a disguise?" Mom countered. "They might want to rob us or kill us. I think those are the same people who are listening in on my phone."

"Why would someone want to hurt us?" Jane and I asked, disregarding the phone comment.

"You're right," Mom conceded. "Go ahead and let them in—I was just kidding."

She laughed it off, and we giggled in return. Because it made sense that Mom was cautious. From the gang shootings to the dead body found in a plastic bin on the neighbor's porch, visiting Mom and Lisa Jean in the house I grew up in was always an adventure.

I convinced myself that she was fine.

2004: Who Needs Alcohol Anyway?

Much hustle and bustle ensued as the family gathered to celebrate Thanksgiving. Excited chatter rang through the small house as food was prepared and seating was arranged for the twenty guests milling from room to room.

It was hard to imagine ten people once coexisting here, with only three bedrooms, a cramped kitchen, and a living/dining room barely large enough to hold a pool table. Fortunately, we'd never had the luxury of a pool table, because then *we* wouldn't have fit.

Returning now for the holiday, we nestled like happy sardines into the confined space, basking in the warmth of familiarity.

"Mom," queried Denise, our fourth oldest sibling, "where are the rest of the plates and drinking glasses? I can't find them in the cupboard and we need them for the meal."

"Don't be silly," replied Mom. "We aren't missing anything."

"I'll look," offered Marie, the oldest. "Denise is right: You don't have all the dishes you normally have."

Mom ignored them.

So we did what true Catholic families do: We sacrificed. We didn't pour any drinks that day. (Swigging from the bottle, however, was a different story).

Christmas Day, we gathered again.

Mark (my third oldest brother) and Derrick (the oldest of all) spread out on the couch to watch the football game.

Clank.

Mark's heels backed into the missing dishes. Someone had shoved them, dirty, under the couch.

A hushed silence filled the room. Had Lisa Jean done this, or Mom?

Denial is a blissful blanket of protection against the raw biting teeth of reality. After much debate behind Mom's back, we decided Lisa Jean must have done it. That made more sense to everybody.

Except for Lisa Jean.

"I did not do that!" Lisa Jean declared adamantly. "Mom did. I do my own dishes!"

Hmmm...

The rest of us eyed each other with a blend of humor and confusion.

2005: Sleuthing and Confrontation

The phone rang.

"Hi, Joan. This is Daniel, your mom's neighbor. I thought I saw your mom outside last night dressed all in black. She seemed to be hiding from someone. I can't swear it was her, but it was someone of her size and stature."

I hung up the phone.

"Mom, were you outside last night?" I asked.

"Yes," she said. "I was bringing in the trash cans."

"Were you doing anything else?"

"No, but I think someone was trying to saw into my house."

Say what?

"*Saw* into your house?" I said. "Why would you think that?"

"Never mind," she said quickly. "Sorry, I was confused—I think I saw that on a TV show last night."

Suddenly, I felt like the crazy one.

The voices in some family members' heads told us something was wrong. The utterances in other minds said Mom was fine.

Clutching the thin veil of hope that we in the former group were wrong, we approached her with tenderness.

"Mom, are you okay?" I asked.

"We think you are acting confused and forgetting things," Denise added. "We think you should go see a doctor."

Mom's fangs of rebuttal tore through our hearts, disguised as anger and silence. That was her only defense against losing what was slipping away: her mind. She bit back and would not talk to some of us for months.

2006: The Verdict

The evaluation showed early stages of Alzheimer's. Symptoms included confusion, memory loss, spatial disorientation, and paranoia.

Mom stood tall and accepted her fate. She gave away her car. She invited us to a course called *The Basics: Memory Loss, Dementia & Alzheimer's*. We attended, armed with love and sadness. Mom was the strongest of us all.

Alzheimer's is like tripping down the stairs. As you slowly descend, you suddenly stumble and topple. The change is abrupt and you plummet hard. You can never go back to where you started, but you *can* keep falling.

My siblings and I were inflicted with some of the same symptoms as Mom:

1. Confusion: How could *you*, the strong and physically healthy one, be diagnosed with such a tragic disease? You, the generous, caring, loving woman who raised us?

2. Paranoia: Fear of what lay ahead for Mom, for Lisa Jean, her dependent daughter, and for all of us. How could the rest of us take adequate care of both of them? How would we manage?

3. Memory Loss: We tried to forget the pain we were experiencing day to day, watching Mom slowly slip away.

We all rallied, helping out with finances, managing L.J.'s care, seeking medical advice, and more.

In some ways, Lisa Jean became Mom's caretaker—her memory.

"Where did I put my glasses?"

"They're on your head."

"Did I lock the door?"

"I did it for you."

Watching the bond between the two grow as their roles suddenly reversed was both heartbreaking and uplifting. The magnitude of Lisa Jean's ability to be there for Mom reverberated through all our souls.

2010: The Battle Intensifies

It happened: the frantic phone call, pleading for salvation.

"I'm scared," Mom cried. "You need to come now."

"Scared of what?"

"It's not right," Mom said. "You have to help me. Please, please help me."

The Tormentor

Mark rushed to Mom's house to be with her and Lisa Jean, and then we moved them into my house until we could find help.

Mom's mind tripped deeper into the darkness. She saw bugs on the bedspread. She used travel documents for our Uganda trip as dishes for the salad. She screamed in the night at monsters that were not there. The Tormentor rendered her unable to care for herself or Lisa Jean.

She was no longer the mother we knew—sturdy as an oak tree, bright and strong. She was but a husk, her mind shedding its weight for a winter of loss, her thoughts dropping like acorns in autumn, memories fluttering in the wind. Her thoughts were the leaves of the tree, musings that varied in color, shape, and clarity—some curled and brown, some torn and holey. They clung to her branches in hopes of survival, but the law of nature swept them away, the winds of time creating a vortex of confusion and chaos, stripping her of all pride and pluckiness.

This winter of the frozen mind lasted thirteen long years, each more bone-chilling and bitter than the last.

If Mom could have expressed her thoughts, I know she would have said: "The Tormentor will shed me of my mental and physical presence. I will travel in and out of my own reality, showing glimpses of the me you used to know, all the while shouting: 'Don't give up on me!' Those may not be my exact words—they may come out in an angry roar or a clawing of hands. I am living a life you just can't see. I'll fight you when I don't know I'm fighting. Please know I love you more than my scream of anguish or my punch of rebellion will ever say. The pain I caused was never personal to you but very personal to me."

Mom's mind became the theater of war and her body a citadel. The film in her head rolled on as she fought thieves, talking horses, and dragons—her cane an imaginary sword and her legs striking out at attackers that were invisible to us.

If we could have charged in like Luke Skywalker or Wonder Woman, we would have beheaded her demons. But we didn't have those types of weapons; we had only our love and our best intentions.

Mom, I'm sorry, I'm so sorry.

Florence Nightingale

Despite being unable to care for herself, Mom found ways to take care of others. After a hard fall, she lay on the emergency room table with a cracked-open head.

I called her on the phone, hacking and coughing with the flu.

"I am sorry you fell," I said.

"You don't sound so good," she replied. "Are you okay? Are you taking care of yourself?"

She was always Florence Nightingale, thinking only of others.

I read aloud to her *Tuesdays with Morrie: An Old Man, a Young Man, and Life's Greatest Lesson*, described as "A wise and loving story that teaches us those things we ought to know already, but have somehow forgotten" (Rev. L. Annie Forester, Minister Emerita, *Goodreads*).

In the book, Mitch takes care of Morrie who has Lou Gehrig's disease. He feeds Morrie, reads to him, and rubs his back, arms, and legs. Inspired by Mitch's role model as a caregiver, I, too, wanted to show I cared.

"Mom, may I massage you?" I asked.

"Hmmmm," she sighed.

I took that as a "Yes, I'd love for you to do that." With a feathery touch, I kneaded her bird-like arm.

Seconds passed. "You can stop that now," she whispered tenderly.

"The Tormentor will destroy you and often the relationships around you."

A hospice worker told us that as the disease progresses, families either grow closer together or further apart. Forgiveness, perseverance, love, and understanding are the glue that helps everyone grow closer.

Mom,

With gentle intention, you taught me to do what was best for you, not for me.

2011: Three Halves Don't Make a Hockey Whole

Like Hockey, Alzheimer's is divided into three parts: the early stages, the middle stage, and the late stages. Hockey is referred to as having "three halves." I think whoever said that had Alzheimer's.

The Alzheimer's game can be one of passes, fumbles, body-checking, head-butting, interference, breaking a stick, and getting back up and trying again. It's often filled with players, coaches, and an audience yelling: "Thank you for all you are doing!" "Do it this way!" "You fucked up!" "What were you thinking?" "Good job." "Save my ass!" "I don't want to be sued."

The whole time, the players and family members are fighting, fighting, fighting to participate in a game that can't be won. At least not in the way anyone wants.

The loved ones learn that they can survive, can grow, can live and learn. The end goal is not to win. It's to do the best at caring for the person you love without losing yourself in the process. And that's not a game at all—it's a journey. This individual once took care of you; now it's your turn to give back.

There was no blue line defining which stage Mom was in, but I found the middle stage to be the hardest, because, as is typical, it lasted the longest. Mom was less able to communicate; she was withdrawn, sometimes violent, and at increased risk of hurting herself.

The three halves left a lot of holes: holes in our hearts, a cavernous feeling of loss, gaps in relationships. Thank heavens for the professional caregivers who filled the orifices in the fractured world that was convulsing beneath our feet.

2012: Forks and Foxes

We were seeing red. We followed what felt like the Yellow Brick Road (though in this case, it was grey) through the large installation entitled *Fox Games* by Sandy Skoglund. Pushing Mom in her wheelchair through this art museum exhibit, I was unsure of what she could grasp, questioning if she was even enjoying the outing.

We were submerged into a red room resembling a fifteen-foot car tunnel, which was besieged by one red fox, twenty-seven grey foxes, and a squirrel, all hopping, bouncing, and prancing on dozens of chair-surrounded tables set with forks and knives, salt and pepper shakers, breadbaskets, and plastic flowers.

Mom had been quiet for over two hours. But she said loud and clear: "This is one place I wouldn't want to eat dinner." Then she went mute.

I laughed and laughed as I silently cried to know that my mother was still in there. My lesson learned on that outing was one of hope.

> *Mom,*
>
> *You gave me the ability to love what was not. You gave me signs and humor to hold on to as the journey got rougher. You reminded me of the "It Makes Me Eat My Young" story and Lisa Jean. How funny it was to have knives, forks, and foxes create laughter once again.*

2013: A Sea of Confusion

The Tormentor preys on a person, seeping like billows of smoke under their bones.

This voyage is on uncharted seas, aboard a vessel adrift in waves of uncertainty that lift caregivers and family members and slam them against the rocks, leaving them battered and bruised.

Lacking experience in a storm so fierce, each proposes to steer the ship their own way. Opinions and emotions pelt the journey like hail from an angry sky, adding to the turbulence of the waters. Some may feel on trial for crimes they did not commit, while others may lack the emotional fortitude to face this difficult challenge head-on.

Clinging desperately to one another to survive this merciless tempest, each person lives in his or her own squall. *Where is the anchor? God, I don't know, I don't know, I don't know.*

Thankfully, in time, the storm will calm and love will prevail.

But right now, the Tormentor was steering our ship and mutiny was at hand, sucking the life out of Mom and those around her.

2014: Another Sinking Ship

I cried most of October of 2014 because yet another ship began to sink, and no rowboat or life preserver was going to save anyone on that craft. Lisa Jean became violent and combative, and we learned that she, too, had Alzheimer's.

I sent out flares and cried out in desperation. But many I'd counted on paid me no mind. Not out of spite, but out of uncertainty or powerlessness.

My S.O.S. did not go completely unheeded; other friends, family, and professionals threw out lifelines to Mom, Lisa Jean, me, and our siblings. They were our cheerleaders. They gave us determination when it felt easier to give up. They were there when I wished the disease would take me rather than my having to watch it take the ones I loved. These hardships bonded me closer to others and made me a stronger oar in the rough seas.

I learned I could depend on those I least expected, like the government employees who worked beyond the call of duty purely out of love for Lisa Jean and people like her. Other folks came to the rescue by playing therapist and listening to my struggles over and over. One friend shared stories about her own sibling with Down syndrome. Another who was struggling with cancer, Tamara Blett, shared her book *Awakening Your Powers of Coping and Healing*. "It doesn't matter if it's a terminal illness, the death of a loved one, an unwanted diagnosis of cancer, or a tragic accident leaving you paralyzed," she taught me. "You have the power to cope."

- You have control of your thoughts.
- You have power over your health and well-being.
- Let friends and family help.
- Now is where you are, always.

Alzheimer's caused many casualties: Relationships died from the strain; happiness and hope were lost; friendships tired of the prolonged sadness. Yet out of those losses came much positive: I learned the power of love.

Strength in Numbers

My mom's strength came in God. My strength came in my love for Mom and Lisa Jean. It also came from knowing that this journey was like an in-flight emergency: I had to put on my own oxygen mask before taking care of them.

None of us trains for difficulties in life, but strength eventually comes from reaching deep down within ourselves to tap into qualities we didn't know we had. It comes in the form of tenacity: We keep trying and learning, and we don't give up. We love with the intensity and power of a tsunami; it's all we have. In life, there's no coin toss to decide who gets the first kick. There are no replays and no referees to say if you did it right or wrong (though many *would* presume to both judge and penalize!). This is no true game.

I used the **Gorilla Glue** in my MANEtain Toolbox. I set boundaries to stop the spread of the problem. I fixed my mind on the positives in life. I cemented my resolve to be there for Mom and Lisa Jean.

The Tormentor

Mom's favorite poem, "Footprints in the Sand," reminded me that I never had to do this alone.

Footprints in the Sand

One night I dreamed a dream.
I was walking along the beach with my Lord.
Across the dark sky flashed scenes from my life.
For each scene, I noticed two sets of footprints in the sand,
one belonging to me and one to my Lord.
After the last scene of my life shot before me,
I looked back at the footprints in the sand.
There was only one set of footprints.
I realized that this was at the lowest
and saddest times of my life.
This always bothered me
and I questioned the Lord about my dilemma.
"Lord, you told me when I decided to follow You,
You would walk and talk with me all the way.
But I'm aware
that during the most troublesome times of my life,
there is only one set of footprints.
I just don't understand why, when I need You the most,
You leave me."
He whispered, "My precious child, I love you
and will never leave you, never, ever,
during your trials and testings.
When you saw only one set of footprints,
it was then that I carried you."

—Margaret Fishback Powers

The weight of Alzheimer's was heavy for Mom, Lisa Jean, me, and all those around us. While I couldn't stop the disease, I could seek out support from those who could help me hold it together: doctors, nurses, support staff, hospice workers, friends, family…all amazing in their own way. Thank heavens there were a lot of gorillas in that glue, because I needed all the help I could get.

And we took turns carrying each other along the way.

Stop This Ride; I Want to Get Off

Seeing Mom slumped in her bed, face slack, right side even more wilted than usual, we rushed her to the ER, thinking she might be having a stroke.

"When did this happen?" asked the intake nurse.

"How long has she been lethargic?" demanded the doctor.

"Emma, can you hear me?" they asked her. "Emma, lift your right hand."

Mom endured an MRI, blood tests, X-rays, and a team of eight doctors and students poking and prodding her. That ER doc led her team of medical professionals as if she were the hero in this story, with only distant concern for her patient, the valiant warrior.

After seven hours of doctors acting like Mom was their lab experiment, she tired of them riding in on their Steed of Hope, offering a respite from death.

"Mom," I said, "you didn't have a stroke. You have been such a good patient."

"Thank you," she replied in a meek voice. "I don't mean to be."

2015: Butterfly Kisses

Mom,

I cocooned myself around your frail body that posed as a hanger for your loose, wrinkled skin. I was the cloak that held no power to shield you from the frigid invisible intruder. You ate the poison apple and the toxins seeped into your core like carbon monoxide. We searched for remedies and concoctions to break the ugly curse placed on both you and L.J. It didn't exist. We served up love potions from our own hearts to stop the decay. We sought Prince Charming in the guise of doctors, to stop the unstoppable. But no love's first kiss could bring you back to us.

My last kiss to you was a good-bye kiss. You gave into the Tormentor on June 14, 2015. You released yourself from the pain, developing wings to soar.

Today, I feel your presence when I see a butterfly, one of your favorite creatures on Earth.

Living Out a Life Sentence

We, the ones who are here taking care of the ones on the sinking ship, are like stars in a vast sea of darkness.

Keep twinkling, keep shining. Be there as long as your loved one is devoted to each breath. Commit to sailing; not sinking yourself. If you can measure your voyage against others' hardships—corruption, malaria, poverty, malnutrition—perhaps you will feel less victimized.

If you are the patient, create a contract with those involved in your care before things get bad. Visit Caregiver.com for ideas on how to manage money and family. Set boundaries in this game that is not a game at all. The field is your home, the nursing home, or the hospital.

As a primary caregiver, be sure to take breaks. Leave the playing field. Give to yourself. Take care of yourself. Rely on friends and family. Don't beat yourself up when you fumble. Get a spine. Protect yourself from pain by letting in only what matters. Remember: Doctors don't know everything, though some will act as though they do. The doctors and nurses who don't presume to be omniscient are the key to your sanity.

I'VE NEVER MADE A MISTAKE...

A nurse herself, Mom was a model of mettle.

Dear Mom,

Your children survived your life sentence by virtue of the love you and Dad gave us growing up. You set our foundation by embedding roots as the oak tree standing strong for us when we were weak. You built a bond amongst us all that in your loss speaks louder than words.

As your children, we, too, learned to withstand any tribulation, through the tenacity you displayed and the mentors you and Dad became. You embraced diversity and we now live that lesson. Humor, love, and laughter are the threads that bind us.

Today, even though you are gone, we know you are here in spirit. And you are telling us that no matter how bad things get, to love and accept each other for who we are. Because our intentions are good and each of us is doing the best we can with what we have—even if that means we are sinking when we are supposed to be the life preserver.

Your disease was like a mountain crumbling into the ocean: slow and painful with shock waves reverberating across the continents. It was a life sentence with no parole. But you handled the mental incarceration with humor and grace.

You guided us on what to tell others and how to handle the progression of your disease. This included a deep wisdom and acceptance that it might be best to place you in a facility so no resentment would build amongst us and all would be happy with the care provided. However, we weren't willing to concede this. You deserved to stay in your home.

Mom, your Alzheimer's crashed our reality, uninvited. Slowly, inwardly you left us. But you invited us to join you on your journey—right up until the Tormentor grasped your hand a final time and led you away from us. When you look back and see sets of footprints in the sand, I hope that you'll find it was us, your daughters and sons, who carried you with our love.

You are still here. We are still here!

We love you forever, your children

19

WAIT, WAIT— DON'T SHOOT!

Grief Can Be a Loaded Gun

Hidden in the shadows, the figure cloaked in mystery twitches and tenses. As labored Darth-Vader breathing escapes its core, hands reach…for what???? A tremor ripples through the hunched form. Drug-induced? Mentally ill? Armed and dangerous?

Hand on his weapon, ready to defend his nation, the linebacker-large security guard barks menacingly at the villain in the Volkswagen rental car: "What do *you* need?"

The scrappy little nothing in the VW Bug—all one hundred and fifteen pounds of her—sobs in defeat. "I— I need you to be nice to me."

The guard takes a deep breath and gently coaxes the weepy wet rag out of her meltdown.

"Let's start over," he says. "You see, I didn't know what you were reaching for in your purse. What is your name?"

"Joan," I say through hyperventilating inhales. I sound like I'm wearing a scuba regulator. "I'm lost," I mewl while blowing my nose. "I've been driving around in circles for an hour–*blubber, blubber, honk!*"

The guard looks at me kindly. "I'm Charles," he says. "Why don't you pull over and come in to the guardhouse. I'll take a look at the address you're trying to get to. Where are you from?"

"I'm from Colorado," I explain. "We're moving to Washington, D.C., and I'm house-hunting. I'm supposed to pick up my three-year-old, but I can't find my way back to the hotel."

I snivel between short *I-can-do-this, I-can-do-this, I-can-stop-crying* breaths, my heart slowing to a gentle roar.

"Joan, it's nice to meet you," he says. "How did you end up here, at the entrance to the Pentagon?"

"*I don't knowwwwww,*" I whimper, my small intakes of air now chasing each other. Tears flow freely, my mascara spider-legging down my cheeks to pool at my chin in the shape of a black goatee.

"I'm here to assist," says Charles, handing me a tissue. "You stand here, and I'll figure out where you need to go."

"Thank you," I reply, mentally repeating the triumph of the day: *He didn't shoot me, he didn't shoot me.* At the same time realizing that Charles' mantra must be: *She didn't shoot me, she didn't shoot me.*

"The directions are written on this piece of paper," he says. "Can I do anything else for you? Are you okay to drive?"

"No, yes, I am calm now. I'm sorry I frightened you. It didn't occur to me that *I* could be scary to *you*. Of course you couldn't know I was searching for an address in my bag and *not* a gun."

"Joan, you have a nice day and good luck."

I walk to my car and just as I open the car door, Charles calls out with good intentions: "It can't be all that bad."

I burst into tears. "I lost my baby."

Then I drive away.

Sucker-Punched

One may think this emotional tsunami happened days after I lost Eliza, or maybe a month. The reality is that Allen was offered a temporary job in D.C. fourteen months after Eliza's loss. We decided that moving for a year might do us good.

Heartache can sucker-punch you when you least expect it. You think you are fine, that you have your emotions under control and have moved on. Or at least that your daily crying jags are now a thing of the past.

There is no right or wrong way to grieve. In fact, when I stopped crying every day, I thought I would forget Eliza. I couldn't have been more wrong.

You can't predict when or how grief will grip you in a Darth-Vader chokehold, leaving you out of control, gasping in a puddle. You may look like you chopped ten onions as you watch your waterworks overflow Lake Michigan. That is okay.

Your Emotions Can Turn on A Dime

The vacuum salesclerk may have to supply you with a box of tissues; the sight of a little girl in a pink tutu might reduce you to nothing; or hearing a certain song may buckle your knees because it was your father's favorite. A lacrosse stick could spark the idea that had your son lived, he might have been the star player on the high school lacrosse team. Or the color purple might rattle your bones because it reminds you of your mother-in-law and the Raging Grannies group she was so active in. Because you are not in your right mind, you might wipe your tears and blow your nose on a complete stranger's sleeve.

Embrace that bleak visitor and be okay letting her out of Pandora's Box. Now, if you meltdown daily because your banana won't peel with grace, or convulse at the deli counter because the meatloaf isn't on sale, and you continue this for years on end, embracing "Cry Me a River" as your theme song, then it might be time to seek professional help. Otherwise, accept that you'll have good days and bad days, and that eventually the good days will outnumber the bad.

Just as your emotions can turn to sadness, you can find small ways to honor and remember the ones you've lost. Some feel uplifted by seeing a hawk or a butterfly, or by a snowball plopping on their head while thinking about their son. Inspired by a poem my friend wrote for another friend who had lost her husband, I find solace in dimes that mysteriously appear in the most poignant places.

Dimes
by Margot Burns

I see them everywhere now.
Our daughters too, so strong and beautiful, missing you.
They found one on the track
that wraps around the schoolyard,
and then another under the antique oak table at the Lodge—
our sanctuary while you were in hospice.

Did I ever tell you the story?
It was my friend Kim.
A connection from home
and a welcome friend when I moved to California.
Just before her grandmother died,
she gave Kim a jar of dimes—an odd collection.
When Kim's mother died years later,
dimes started appearing.

Wait, Wait—Don't Shoot!

Shiny distractions from her grief.
Comfort tucked away in her pocket.

I found one
the morning I lost you.
The glint of it catching my eye,
nestled along the edge of the cemetery.
I was there to pick out your plot,
awash with the surreal absurdity of it,
to make this decision on my own,
choosing where I'd leave you to rest.

You'd like it.
Plenty of shade from a giant elm,
and a nice view of the park across the street.
I laid down along the length of your grave,
under the cobalt sky,
a surprising gem on an April day in Iowa,
a stark contrast to the usually dreary grey.
It felt like home.

And now I sit at dinner
with my twin sister and cousin,
at a vineyard in Temecula.
You would have loved it here,
tranquility falling over us
like the soft white clouds
blanketing the mountains.
It rained today,
our anniversary.
Twenty-three years.

I'VE NEVER MADE A MISTAKE...

It was the waitress who discovered the dime under my chair.
She placed it beside me on the table
and the aching for you lifted for a moment.

I long to feel you,
the warmth of your belly pressed against the small of my back,
Lulling me to sleep on a Saturday morning.
Safe in the wrap of your arms.

The dime rests in my hand,
your presence,
a perfect gift.

Today I looked at my brother's memory box my mom made when he died. Shellacked in the box is his dog tag, a picture of Lisa Jean, a card from him, a tissue, a picture of Jesus, and a dime. I'll never know why a dime was so carefully placed in there and entombed for life, but what I do know is I believe in the power of what we do not understand to give us strength.

Light in the Darkness

It's good for people to see you vulnerable. Because Eliza died, I met one of my closest friends.

Bob was enrolled in a Tiny Tots gymnastics class when I was pregnant with Eliza. Another mother and I had chatted casually in the months leading up to her birth date. And all the parents in attendance had seen my belly grow and grow.

The day I showed up with no belly and no baby was one of the hardest days of my life. I thought I was strong enough to take him back to class without crying.

I was wrong.

This woman enveloped me in kindness. She lifted me up when I was at my lowest. Although that was twenty-two years ago, I still cry when I think of that day. During those dark times, she was a lighthouse beaming me home.

It's My Tuna Wrap and I'll Cry If I Want To

When you think you finally have grief by the balls and you can't be sucker-punched because you have matured and learned all there is to know about grief management, try ordering a tuna wrap.

Two years ago, I was meeting a friend for dinner and she was running late. I ordered a tuna lettuce wrap and a glass of wine. As I waited for both my friend and my appetizer, I reflected on the sheer impotence of my situation. My mom was physically alive but mentally not the mother I knew—by now, she could no longer identify me. And with Lisa Jean's diagnosis of Alzheimer's, my entire family was boxed in by an unjust set of circumstances called life.

"Here you go, Ma'am," said the young-enough-to-be-my-son waiter as he set my wrap in front of me.

"Thank you," I blurted, tears bursting down my cheeks.

The *OMG-what-do-I-do?* look in the waiter's face told me that his How to Be a Superstar Waiter training manual hadn't included a section on "Actions to take if your customer breaks down crying when you serve her a tuna lettuce wrap."

I looked up at him, wiped my nose on the monogrammed restaurant napkin, and said: "I love tuna. I love tuna *soooooo*, so much."

He sighed, I sighed, and we both laughed. Then I apologized and explained that my mother was dying.

"I'm sorry for your pain," he said. "Thank you for making an awkward moment light."

If you are the one bawling in your Thom Yum Soup, explain as much as you feel comfortable to the one watching. People can handle your breakdowns—even strangers. Don't beat yourself up. Apologize if you must, but do it only once.

Onlookers may be speechless, confused, and possibly a bit uncomfortable, but remind yourself that it could be worse: You could be asking them to pay for your therapy. If you are the one intercepting the tears, do your best to reassure the blubberer that you are okay and you are sorry for their sadness.

Rinse, Cry, and Spit

No matter why your heart is broken, sorrow can be like carbon monoxide: invisible, colorless, odorless, and toxic. And if left unchecked, it can be deadly. Traces remain hidden in your soul, hovering over your heart waiting to lunge.

Sadness shows up unannounced and uninvited, and can hit you with the force of a firing gun. And it doesn't care if you are amidst making one of the most major decisions of your life, such as whether to buy purple cabbage or Cheetos.

You may walk into the dentist's office as your own bubbly babe, light on your feet, singing "Feeling Groovy." You plop into the examination chair as chipper as a beaver who has just two front teeth and a free supply of dental floss.

The dental hygienist who greets you doesn't notice you're not alone. Your sidekick is despair, seeking not to hurt you but to find some release—steadfastly waiting for the right Tigger-trigger, to pounce.

As your teeth are cleaned, your thoughts wander, bereavement leading them to that corner of your mind where the memories of your loved one are tucked away. The dental hygienist asks you to wash away the strawberry/root-beer/mint-flavored mouthwash.

And that does it.

Grief, who had been sitting silently with you in the dentist's chair, unleashes its misery. Bursting into tears, your bubbly-beaver self becomes a blubbering baboon.

Worry not. You are human. You shall overcome.

So go ahead: *Rinse, cry, and spit.* *RINSE, CRY, and SPIT.* It will cleanse not only your mouth, but your soul.

20
MUSIC GAVE SPEECH TO MY ANGEL

A Dance-Date With Destiny

This was it. This promised to be more exciting than Brad Pitt showing up at my house with an industrial-sized barrel of coconut oil; more nerve-wracking than finding out Angelina Jolie was hot on the trail of Brad and his money and coming to my humble abode to collect; and scarier than Jennifer Aniston finding out it was *her* coconut oil Brad was going to use on me.

I had a dream, and in a few short days it would become a reality. In the past, I had come close, and every time it fell through, I was like an addict denied a fix. I wallowed, I cursed, I felt sorry for myself. I donned my snorkel, facemask, and flippers and went deep into my sewage pool of disappointment. I spent much more time there than in my kiddie pool of happiness.

This time, though, it was gonna happen.

With the big event a week away, Fabio became a regular visitor, crawling into my mind and robbing me of my orgasm of sleep. I let fear of what could go wrong overshadow the possibility of perfection. Lisa Jean was involved, so anything could happen. What if I had to do our "catch and release" routine in front of sixteen hundred people?

Fueled by Franti

Let me back up.

Michael Franti and his band, Spearhead, had been with me since 1994. Their spirit and their songs had carried me through the ultimate sorrows. After Eliza died, their encouraging words "Of course you can" held me up when I all I wanted to do was fold, shrivel away, and disappear.

Their hopeful lyrics guided me through my nine miscarriages, assuring me: "A baby's love leaves fingerprints upon the heart."

I'd found support through humming their lines "I know, I know, I know I'm not alone," as I tried to figure out whose mind was slipping more: my sister's or my mom's. This, after finding the dishes stowed under the couch and a St. Christopher medal in the hide-a-key box outside. The house key previously stashed there became one of the treasures Mom buried in the yard, perhaps in hopes of someone digging their way to it from China—Asian warriors covered in earth, rising to unlock her mind and free her from the disease of Alzheimer's.

The beat of Spearhead reminding me that "everything is possible" fueled my continued search for the reason I couldn't sleep, sit, or stand without feeling like a semi had parked on my midriff as the undetected umbilical hernia silently shredded my abdominal wall. It kept my tears at bay when the chronic pain felt worse than giving birth to Chewbacca with a porcupine afro.

Rock-'n'-Roll: Our Saving Grace

My steady companion on this rockin' and rollin' journey was my sister Lisa Jean, who—despite her Down syndrome and OCD diagnoses—connected with Franti's lyrics.

Shaped like an Oompa-Loompa sporting a few extra pounds, Lisa moved her booty as if she were Edyta Sliwinska from *Dancing with the Stars*. Our dance floor was her bedroom's shag carpet and our adoring audience, our reflections in the full-length mirror affixed to her closet door.

L.J. truly had the rhythm of saints. Together we weebled and wobbled and never fell down—neither physically nor emotionally—while singing and dancing.

"They say that miracles are never ceasing," crooned Michael.

"Yeah!" Lisa Jean hooted as she dipped and twirled.

"Don't give up on me; I won't give up on you," Michael encouraged.

"Okay!" Lisa Jean and I agreed.

For years and years, Lisa and I danced in her nine-by-thirteen-foot bedroom—popping, hopping, locking, and gyrating body parts in ways no one but Lisa Jean could.

Michael Franti & Spearhead's lyrics gave our souls wings to soar above the weight of life.

I'VE NEVER MADE A MISTAKE...

A Fading Star

Lisa Jean was my superstar. But her stage light was dimming. Now in her forties, she was responding less and less to music.

By this time, our mom had advanced to Stage 3 Alzheimer's. Like an aging canine, Mom was unable to speak except with her big brown eyes. You could feel her will, but her body was unable to share her thoughts or move on her own. She was asleep more than awake. I wanted to hold her frail, boney body and bring back to life that spunky young pup I once knew as my mother.

That's when we were dealt the next devastating blow. That's when Lisa Jean was diagnosed with Alzheimer's, too.

L.J. shut down, and like Helen Keller, communicated mostly physically, through angry and aggressive behaviors. She required constant supervision and became a danger to herself and others. She paced like a caged animal, tried to exit moving cars, and increased her use of The Plop. Whenever she didn't like what she was being asked to do, she sat down and refused to move—be it in the street or the entrance to McDonald's. And she could stay in one spot for up to three hours.

It just wasn't fair.

How can the world be just when some people aren't given a fighting chance at birth? Why are some born with neurons and brain cells marching along like a well-tuned band while others start their first day of life with suicide bombers obliterating nerve cells that would have enabled them to live independently, go to college, have children, and be accepted in society for who they are rather than who they are not?

And after all we'd already been through, the universe had hit the Repeat button on our family. Just as we were watching our beloved mother spiral downward, our sister was facing the same fate.

Lisa Jean is a person with Down syndrome, not a Down syndrome person. Still, with the effects of Alzheimer's piled on top of that and her OCD, she was now losing her sight and her ability to communicate; plus, her anxiety was increasing. Music could no longer coax her out of her mental prison.

I was inconsolable. Abject despair became an unwanted squatter in my soul, sending fear and sorrow tearing through my heart, producing bouts of sobbing that ruled my body like an alpha dog leading a hunt. I wanted the long-drawn blackness to take me someplace where all our pain would cease.

But I knew I had a choice: I could entrench myself in the darkness or I could find the light. I decided to follow Mom's path. In my position, she would have focused on the life left in all of us, rather than the injustice of it all.

The more Mom and Lisa Jean deteriorated, the more I sought out Michael Franti's music to fuel my drive to thrive. His words "I believe in the power of positivity. What we think, listen to, and believe all affect the way we feel every day" echoed in my head as I fought to ensure that my mother's and sister's needs were met.

The Dream, the Impossible Dream

My dream actually had three layers to it.

1. To see Spearhead in concert.

2. To meet Michael Franti in person.

3. For Lisa Jean to meet Michael.

My first try at the first layer was in 2001, but it didn't get far. I skipped the concert because I had GAS: I volunteered to drive a vehicle-void friend out to a dinner with other mutual friends…a dinner I was not invited to! In 2005, I finally made it to a concert—Phase 1 complete. But when Michael invited members of the audience up onstage, my daughter and I were stopped just before mounting the stairs—we were so close! My third concert opportunity came and went in 2008, as I was entrenched in caring for my mom and Lisa Jean.

In February of 2014, Phase 2 of my fantasy finally came true: I met the entire band! J Bowman, Michael's lead guitarist, made it so. A true megastar, he took a chance on me, a complete stranger.

The band was playing at an outdoor venue in Vail, Colorado. I had hoped to bring Lisa with me but she wasn't available.

When the concert ended, Michael, who usually greets the crowd, hobbled immediately off stage because he was on crutches with a hurt knee. J took Michael's place, and with his natural flare, charmed those of us who had gathered at the edge of the stage. My daughter, Anna, her friend, and I got our picture taken with him. Then, with fear shouting in my ear *Don't do it!* I gathered up enough nerve to tell J about my children's book *Slumps, Bumps, and Triumphs*, which I had written and illustrated to provide readers of all ages with whimsical problem-solving skills to help them overcome the hardships of life. I asked him if I could talk to Michael about sharing the book with people in need, such as supporters and members of Michael and his wife, Sara's, foundation, "Do It For The Love."

The Do It For The Love Foundation's goal is to "grant live concert music wishes to people living with life-threatening illnesses, children and adults with severe challenges, and wounded veterans, and to provide the opportunity for healing to take place." My hope was to provide those same people with another source of inspiration, in turn giving back to the foundation financially.

"I'll go ask our tour manager," J told me.

Thirty minutes later, he still hadn't returned. So I ditched Anna and her friend to see if I could find him. (In actuality, *they* had abandoned me, citing that I was "embarrassing.") Knees knocking, I mustered up the courage to seek out J again. I went behind the stage, and as fate had it, the Betty White of concert organizers was on my side: She told the security guard trying to stop me that it was okay for me to head into the backstage tent to speak with J.

"Hi, Smurf!" J exclaimed, referring to the layers of clothing I had piled on to steel me from the cold outdoors. "I can't find Michael," he told me, "so follow me."

I did, and he led me up to the band's suite for their concert afterparty! I was in a trance of delight, pinching myself to make sure, *Yes, this is real.* I spoke with Michael, Sara, and the band for about a half-hour. I never did get to discuss my book, but I did get to learn how genuine each and every band member truly is.

Getting to meet Michael *was* a dream come true. But the heartbeat of the dream was missing because Lisa was not there.

It was time for Phase 3.

Doing It For The Love

Hope springs eternal. On December 9, 2015, Michael and J were slated to perform at the famed Ogden Theatre in Denver.

I was seeking solace from my own anguish and relief for Lisa from her inner demons. Maybe this music that had touched our lives so often could get through to her. So this time, I applied for tickets to the show for both Mom and Lisa through the Do It For The Love Foundation, based upon their special needs. Sadly, Mom died before the event.

The regal invite came via email. Our presence was kindly requested to hear the dynamic duo Michael and J in concert.

My reaction? Like a cow being tipped, I froze. After that, I vacillated from being overjoyed to scared poop-less. My STDs flared as I worried about this all going as planned. Yet my GAS syndrome urged me: *Do it for Lisa Jean.*

So I RSVP'd yes and invited L.J.'s caregivers and a few special friends and family along.

That's when my GAS went full-blown—I like to think in a good way. Weeks before the event, I took out my MANEtain Toolbox and used tool number 4: I created a **Battle Plan.** Using tool 2, **Hairnet,** I researched the logistics of parking, meeting points, handicapped accessibility, and seating. I mailed gifts (made by the women in Uganda) to the staff of the Do It For The Love Foundation to thank them for their kindness. I prepared gifts made by these same ladies to take to the concert for Michael and J. I also purchased food I knew they liked.

As I was waiting, I tossed and turned each night from fear of the unknown. This felt riskier than peeking into Matt Lauer's office closet. I had to kick Fabio out of bed over and over because I was exhausted. I used tool 8: I embraced change. I also used tool 12: I waited and did nothing.

The Royal We

The day of the concert was finally upon us. When we arrived, we were treated like royalty. Queen Elizabeth herself would have been jealous. Our throne was the handicapped section of the theater, which we shared with two other foundation guests—a girl with cerebral palsy and a woman in a wheelchair—along with their family and friends.

Hossein, the band's tour manager, was a king among kings. Despite his obligation to oversee Michael's and J's needs, with genuine compassion and unwavering dedication, he demonstrated what a true nobleman is. He watched over us all like the Royal Guard. And with the patience and understanding of the Dalai Lama, he treated L.J. with the dignity of a princess. Little did we know that Her Highness would be adored by the masses less than two hours later.

When we first sat down, I asked Hossein if Lisa Jean could go onstage.

"Yes," was his reply. "As long as you stay with her." *YIKES.*

As the opening acts played, Lisa Jean got overwhelmed and discombobulated. She shifted in her wheelchair; she cried at the flash of a camera. Finally, she asked to visit the *porcelain* throne. Thankfully, the bathroom was secluded and the noise was manageable. I was grateful I didn't have to resort to asking people not to flush.

After four trips to the silent stalls, Hossein escorted Lisa and me to the bowels of the theater to meet Michael and J. My anxiety heightened. What if Lisa ignored them? What if she did The Plop?!

J greeted us with his effervescent personality.

"Hello, Lisa," Michael said.

Lisa tickled his stomach and squeezed his six-foot-six frame.

"How are you?" he asked.

She tipped off his hat.

Laughter overflowed like champagne being popped.

Grinning, L.J. embraced Hossein.

J enveloped her in love.

We hung out in the dungeon-like room (which was wonderfully tranquil) as the band prepared to go on, and then we watched from the wings of stage left as Michael and J performed.

"It's time," Hossein said to us. "You can go out to be with Michael and J." He motioned us toward the stage.

I held back in the darkness.

"*Oh my, oh no, oh dear,*" I muttered. My heart was throbbing, my mind racing, my palms sweating, and my stomach twisting in knots. Not because of stage fright or being star-struck, but because I was unsure what Lisa Jean would do. What if I had to drag her offstage, wrapping my arms around her like a large catfish being steered into her own swimming hole? That would go over well with the Human Rights Committee.

Self-doubt left me immobilized.

All the World's Her Stage

What happened next, I will never forget.

Like a cat snubbing her nose at dry kibble in search of caviar, Lisa Jean lifted her head and pranced onstage like she was walking on water, leaving me in the dust. As she marched her beautiful booty right to the very front, the crowd exploded. Magic filled L.J.'s entire being and the song "Sound of Sunshine" released it.

Lisa became a cross between twenty Oompa-Loompas and eighteen Edyta Sliwinskas. She wiggled and swayed, shimmied and shook. Her arms were like an octopus on steroids, moving in all directions to the beat of the music. She tossed her short locks about as if they were tresses of gold in a hair conditioner commercial. Her smile stretched from ear to ear, like a Cheshire cat who had found her boundless supply of caviar. Her feet commanded her body, which seemed to be light as a cloud with wisps of air whirling about her, raising her up and twirling her to the pulse of the music.

Michael, J, and the audience had ignited something in her that had long been smoldering. The sea of faces she looked out on embraced her unconditionally. Cell phones lit up as they captured her on film. Hands rose as if reaching for her enchantment. Lisa Jean was the star attraction and she aimed to please.

A volt of confusion surged through me. Who was this beaming ball of energy? Was this cat-like creature the same one who was so often aloof and unreachable? I laughed aloud. Then I teared up and stopped breathing. No longer lost, Lisa Jean was found. In that moment, Lisa and I were alone, flashing back to the happiness and innocence we experienced so many years ago dancing in her room. My chest filled with so much joy, my heart barely had room to beat.

As the song "Say Hey (I Love You)" ended, Lisa bowed and brought her arms over her head full circle as she flicked her hair to infinity.

"Lisa!" Michael yelled, gesturing her over to him.

"Lisa! Lisa!" the crowd started chanting.

"Oh my God!" her caregiver Heidi exclaimed.

"I love you, Lisa!" yelled Kylie, her other caregiver.

Michael cloaked little Lisa in an embrace that rocked the audience to their cores. Their roars of glee bounced off the walls and ceiling. The others onstage, who had come up during one of the many songs Lisa danced to—people who had raised thousands and thousands of dollars for people like Lisa Jean—jumped up and down and enfolded each other in exultation.

Michael's lyrics "I love you, I love you, I love you" were the words I tried to telepathically transmit to each member of the audience. Because every person in the Ogden Theatre that night—Hossein, the security staff, the ticket sellers, the ushers, the light and sound engineers, and the attendees—had changed Lisa's life.

And mine.

Lisa bowed again, as if the spotlight was on her and her alone. Our hearts were on fire. Her own dimming light was now brilliant, and it lit up our lives.

Jedi Mind Flush

As Lisa finished taking her bows, Hossein gently guided us toward stage right… Nope. Lisa wasn't having anything to do with that. She wasn't leaving this party clearly thrown for her. I redirected her stage left, thinking the familiarity might encourage her exit.

And that's when it happened: She did The Plop.

Imagine a large brown bear being hit by a sleeping dart. She embedded the cellulose fibers of her back end into the grains of the stage. Lisa became an immovable force of nature.

Oh no! my mental self-talk screamed. *I'm going to have to go retrieve that Chewbacca I birthed to help get her offstage! The entire* Star Wars *cast will need to bring the Force to move her.*

I didn't want to employ the catch-and-release, which involved my holding on to her like a wrestler from the WWE, because then I'd have to explain to Michael, J, Hossein, *and* the adoring fans why I was sitting on Lisa and that, yes, in fact, she could breathe.

"I'll get you a Dr. Pepper," I offered in a panic.

Nothing.

"Maybe a Subway sandwich?"

No movement.

"I'll take you to the bathroom?"

This she responded to!

I coaxed her up and while our back ends exited, the audience of sixteen hundred applauded.

Two Souls Soothed

As we snaked our way through her admirers, *The Lisa Jean Show* continued.

"You were amazing," said one fan.

"You are a rock star," gushed another.

"Can I have your autograph?" begged a newfound groupie.

During that walk to her throne, over one hundred people complimented Lisa Jean.

But one woman in the waves of admiring strangers stood out. This one directed her enthusiasm at me.

"That was magical," she sighed.

With that, my floodgates of emotion burst and I sobbed a river of tears. All the suppressed stress from the previous years washed from my soul. And this stranger held me so tightly, it was as though Blue the Bear had emerged from the jungles of *Jungle Book* to comfort me and assure me that I was not alone. I will never forget that woman. My sighs of sorrow were released and replaced with relief.

My tears continued to flow as L.J. and I picked our way to our friends. I was held in the arms of Kylie and Heidi, my husband, Allen, and my friends Dana, Maggie, Sarah, and Cara, who all took turns embracing me and sharing their joy. My waterfall streamed endlessly as I floated in a pool of awe. We all cried together, feeling empowered with hope.

L.J. had not danced like that in ten years.

My aspirations of Lisa meeting Michael and J had so greatly exceeded all hope and expectation. It was as though the hands of God had lifted us up and freed us from fear and sorrow and pain. We were like snowflakes, carefree and light, floating on the melody of the band's words and the power of their kindness.

"The experience from the audience was like watching a miracle unfold," Maggie reported to me later. "In a moment, Lisa's dulled eyes became electric and her grin as wide as the stage. We were transfixed. And I couldn't believe Lisa Jean's moves! Damn, that girl's got groove," she gushed. "It was magical, pure bliss."

"After silence," says Aldous Huxley, "that which comes nearest to expressing the inexpressible is music."

The concert gave Lisa Jean expression. And ever since then, she stops and dances to music. She talks more, she is more engaged, and she is more at peace.

Two weeks after the concert, L.J. collapsed and was rushed by ambulance to the ER. We feared she was having a stroke. It was pneumonia. She healed but did not fully recover and she is now on oxygen 24/7. Michael's song "I'm Alive" must be carrying her through. She is thankful for each new day and will let us know so. "I'm alive! I'm alive!" she yells.

Lisa Jean has Down syndrome; she is not Down syndrome. Her charm and gaiety translate to unconditional love, a sense of humor that Kevin Hart would envy, a perception of the world free of judgment, and a defying of gravity with rhythm that would illuminate Michael Jackson's dancing. She has taught me acceptance, patience, kindness, hope, compassion, and more.

Thomas Carlyle famously said, "Music is well said to be the speech of angels."

On the night of December 9, 2015, the beauty of Michael and J's music gave speech to my sister, my angel, Lisa Jean.

21

LAUGH OF THE DAY

Putting the Man Back in Your Mango

Do you ever wish you had more whip in your whipped cream, more cheer in your Cheerios? Do you dream of days when life was not so technologically complicated?

I miss the simple pleasures, like crank phone calls asking, "Is your refrigerator running? You better go catch it." So as not to age myself, I'll clarify that it was me making the call.

I'VE NEVER MADE A MISTAKE...

These days, with caller ID, the vic calls you back and says, *"You'd better run, because when I catch you and your refrigerator, you are going to look like a drone with rump roast in your cockpit."*

I personally enjoy cursing the caller back in turn for bothering me on my landline while I'm simultaneously ironing, closing on a big real estate deal via email, texting the vet, calling the doctor about my pink eye, and Facebooking my daughter's teacher to tell him she has a basketball tournament so therefore she cannot volunteer at the craft fair until an hour later than expected and will also have to leave an hour early to volunteer at the soup kitchen for her student government class. I get to take out my frustrations on a complete stranger whom I bothered first.

I also long for those obscene phone calls: "Your heat expansion excites me. I'll show you my snake. I'm coming, I'm coming." And that's just from the plumber.

He never showed. I think my Meg-Ryan-in-*When-Harry-Met-Sally* response scared him. Usually, the closest I come to heavy breathing is when I get up from watching TV.

A Laugh on Your Behalf

Sometimes I feel my greatest daily accomplishment is getting out of bed and dressed. However, I soon realize that was the easiest part of my day. After managing snot snakes and poop patrol for the gaggle of people and pets in my home, I recognize I'm in a bit of a rut. Let's face it: the fact that my chicken is hand-trimmed has lost its thrill. I no longer find pleasure in my all-in-one shampoo & conditioner that promises to "tousle me softly." I am over counting the spider legs in my recycled toilet paper.

I make a point of mixing up my reality, lest my perspective get plastered into place. I volunteer or travel or change my underwear.

And I come up with something funny every day. I call it my Laugh of the Day. If it's funny enough, I share it with a friend. I now have friends calling to share their own Laugh of the Day.

Yes, Ma'am; No, Man

I seek out laughs from strangers. As I traveled on the train from Washington, D.C., to New York City I asked the ticket collector, "What is the funniest thing you have experienced in your job?"

"When I work the night shift there are lots of prostitutes," he told me. "I went up to one and inquired, 'Ma'am, may I please see your ticket?'

"'*Man?*' She responded. 'You think I'm a man? I'll show you what I am. I ain't no man!'

"She then lifted her skirt, exhibiting her body parts to prove she was indeed a *ma'am*."

The ticket collector paused as I gaped in amazement.

"After that, Joe Schmo, the business traveler, walked up to her and said 'Hello there, fella.'

"Jake the Jock sauntered over and whispered, 'Good evening, dude.'

"Jane the Janitor merrily said, 'Pleased to meet you, bloke.'

"The prostitute then said to Joe, Jake, Jane, and the ticket agent: 'Man, I'm too tired for this.'"

Needling Her Patience

I asked my acupuncturist, "What is the most unusual experience you have had in *your* profession?"

"Sometimes I leave the needles in for a length of time," she explained. "So I left my teenage patient on the table. When I returned twenty minutes later, all I found was a pile of little needles and a note that said, *Gotta run! Thanks.*

"The opposite happened with one of my elderly patients, Rita. I explained to Rita that she was done and free to go. When I came back over an hour later, she was still lying on the table patiently.

"'Why haven't you left yet?' I asked her.

She answered sweetly: 'I thought I still had needles in me.'"

Back-Door Laughs

Due to my years of chronic pain, along with caring for my mom and sister, I've spent a lot of time on the phone with the medical establishment. Sometimes I lose my patience with the prompts, buttons, and being put on hold. One such time, I accidentally discovered that if I cussed at the recorded voice on the other end, I would be immediately transferred to a live person. Try it—it's a good stress release. Simon, the automated greeter for United Airlines, is especially quick to respond.

During my extended stint of suffering, my stomach did its own Cirque du Soleil performance every time I ate. I later found out that was due not only to complications from my umbilical hernia but that I was dairy and gluten intolerant. Previously, I'd been intolerant of those who were food intolerant; after that diagnosis I shut up.

In search of the problem, I had two colonoscopies before the age of fifty. To lighten the mood, I put a sign on my back end that said *Enter Here*. It opened the door, so to speak, for the nurses to laugh. I learned more jokes that day than I had in years.

Lying on the table, I watched the operating room staff hold back giggles while staring alternately at my back end and at my very introverted, conservative doctor. Anticipation was high as the nurses awaited his lifting of the sheet to uncover his personal directives for my procedure.

I passed out from the anesthesia just as I saw him crack a crooked smile. Later, the nurses said his reaction was the highlight of their year.

Based on this grand experience, when I later had knee surgery, I painted my knee to appear bruised and bloodied, and handed out The Far Side cartoons.

My umbilical hernia brought me the pleasure and expertise of many physical therapists over a ten-year period. Our team's process was akin to working in a torture chamber: Pain was inflicted and results were had, but it wasn't fun for any of us.

I brought in a remote-controlled fart machine to fight back.

Phhhh! said my machine as I pushed the remote while Sam adjusted my lower rib cage.

"I'll adjust your neck," Sam said, ignoring the noise.

Mhhhhssspppp! released the hidden apparatus as he loosened up my screaming muscles.

An inquisitive look crossed Sam's face as he continued patiently without uttering a word.

PPPPPHHHPPPMMSS!! blurted the black-box culprit.

"Joan, I think you better have that checked," Sam finally declared.

A Wheezin' to Laugh

The Sound of Home

Just one short sound,
a noise that is known,
a single note,
a tiny tone,
excites my heart.
I feel at home.

Here's your Laugh of the Day: Guess what Daniel Prinzler, the poem's author, is writing about. I'll tell you at the end of this chapter.

Laughs of the Day don't have to consume a lot of energy or take you out of your comfort zone. The little things in life are often the easiest to find humor in—like your lip balm claiming to give you "hope." Thank God it explains *For external use only*.

I also find humor in how others manage stress. My son does back-flips off a tree. The more stress, the more back-flips he does.

Danny's poem is not about the phone ringing and the anticipation of an obscene caller on the other end. It's about my laugh.

My laugh is rather…distinctive. It has been described as the sound of a wild animal, a pig being forced to take a bath, an electric hand-towel dispenser in a bathroom, and a teakettle whistling—all at once. It has caused people to slap me on the back and take me outside for air while handing me an inhaler.

The bonus is that everyone else laughs even harder than I am.

So, if you need more puff in your pastry or man in your mango and an endorphin high, call me and share your Laugh of the Day. You'll hear something akin to an asthmatic hyena. I'll even throw in some heavy breathing to make both you and Meg Ryan happy.

"*YES! YES! YES!*"

22

WALT DISNEY'S COUGH

Expel Your Creative Juices to Take Care of You

What does my creativity have in common with sperm? First of all, I always have countless ideas running amuck. Maybe not 200 million per pop, but more than I can keep up with. From just a single ejaculation, if lined up end to end, both things would stretch six miles. And they just keep coming and coming.

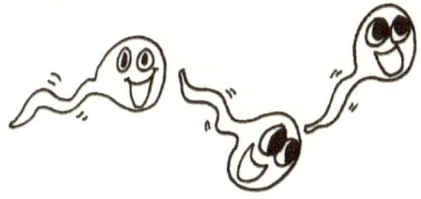

Sperm and my ideas aren't always streamlined; they bob and weave and chase their own tails. And it takes very little foreplay to stimulate my juices. Sperm and my thoughts have a good head near their shoulders.

It's human nature that we're always trying to get ahead. When we aim for a goal, we feel good. We want to give to the world, reproduce. Our creativity needs a release.

Sperm and creative ideas also feel better when free. But although mine are many (ideas, not sperm), few make it to their final destination—in this case, a paint canvas or a book.

My Cup Runneth Over

Unreleased creativity can feel like pent-up sexual tension. Like sperm in a condom, my ideas feel trapped, and I would burst if I had no outlet. That is why I write, paint, and create.

If, in the course of tangibly expressing my thoughts, I can create something beautiful to give to the world, I am even more satiated. Some people are good at math, others at language; my calling is toward creative expression.

My gratification from filling my cup is like a donor's at a sperm bank: I have a purpose, it feels good, and I make a few bucks at it.

The objects of my passion are things I see, hear, and feel daily. They arouse me to erection, spawning the eventual birth of a book, painting, illustration, or presentation. Not all my ideas are the quality of highly sought-after Danish sperm, but at least I have a lot of them. And what a Nordic sperm donor and I do have in common is we tend to be "tall and highly educated, with altruistic motives."

That is why telling tall tales comes naturally to me. Through them, I wish to share the lessons I've learned from my hardships as well as the toughness I have gained. If one seed is planted that inspires growth, beauty, and positive life changes, then all this overflow is worth it.

Contracting the Cough

I am a woman, so you may wonder: Why aren't I using the analogy of eggs rather than sperm? The reason is that women are said to be born with all the eggs they'll ever have. I experienced the pain of that firsthand. While I had a lot of eggs, a lot of them didn't work.

It's different for sperm. They reproduce all day, every day, throughout a lifetime. My brain is the same: it won't stop! This can be a problem, and I have to do repeated "D.O.T. (Don't Over Think) Dumps" when my brain works overtime.

I started motherhood with the goal of running my own business, launching my illustrated characters called The Bird Herd, and working at home to take care of my children. And that worked for a while.

After I had Bob and was pregnant with Eliza, I worked even harder, longer hours, trying to not let the nausea I suffered through the entire pregnancy slow me down.

Shortly after Eliza died, I received an offer from a major company to launch a Bird Herd line of wrapping paper and greeting cards.

But by then, my whole world had shifted. I struggled with the choice of "leaning in" to my career or being there for Bob. Many moms would have been able to manage both, but I couldn't—emotionally or physically. My husband traveled sixty percent of the year for his work, so just making it through the day often felt like too much to handle. In the end, I chose staying at home with my son. I did not pursue the wrapping paper and greeting card offer.

After Eliza died, I worked hard just to breathe as I strove to redefine myself, my family, and my new reality. Many hours and years were spent trying to stay pregnant, searching far and wide for the cure to my mysterious pain, and helping my mother care for Lisa Jean.

I made my bed and accepted lying in it—but not without countless nights with Fabio, my nighttime mind-manipulator, tumbling between the sheets. Feeling imprisoned by some of my choices and with caring for everyone else, I forgot to take care of myself.

That's when I recognized that to avoid wallowing in self-pity, I needed to find a way to channel my ideas—my sperm.

That's when I decided to cough; cough like Walt Disney.

Walking the Walk and Coughing the Cough

Walt Disney's Cough is a spewing of colors, creativity, and characters…a world of imagination, which, like sperm, needs to be controlled and directed. Walt Disney's Cough meant doing something useful, constructive, and concrete with all that activity in my brain.

I am not sure when Walt Disney's Cough started incubating in my system. I don't think I was born with it. It was possibly when my mom or dad read to me in bed, or maybe at the movie theater when I fearfully watched the Evil Queen fall to her death in *Snow White and the Seven Dwarfs*.

Some notable people who have "the Cough" are Jim Henson, Erma Bombeck, A. A. Milne, Michael Franti, J Bowman, and Gary Larson. I'm pretty sure it isn't contagious, but then again, I see many people exhibit the symptoms.

Fortunately, there are methods for coping with Walt Disney's Cough. Instead of stifling your hacks, try directing them toward artistic outlets:

Draw.
Paint.
Write.
Create.
Build.
Sing.
Make Music.
Play.

The Art of Giving—to Me

As the thirty-two-year-old mother of a one-year-old, I struggled with my own "What do I want to be when I grow up?" complex. I asked myself at age forty: "Do I want to be the President of the United States or the Dalai Lama?" At forty-five, I asked: "Do I want to be Picasso, or just sit around looking pretty like the *Mona Lisa*?" At fifty, I asked, "What would Mother Teresa do?" and took my children to Bolivia, Uganda, and El Salvador while creating greeting cards. I wrote/co-wrote and illustrated four children's books (*Peek-A-Boo Who?*; *Bedtime Is for the Birds*; *Slumps, Bumps, and Triumphs*; and *Bye-Bye, Booger Bug: The Art of Nose-Picking*), I painted and sold large canvas paintings, and I performed presentations—all with the help of others helping me to help others.

Now at fifty-nine, I am ready to cough an enormous Walt Disney Cough and share my sperm with others in a big, big way. This book is a start.

How bad is it to have the Cough? Not awful. In fact, it's a relief when I hack. My soul fills with the beauty of the Cough rather than the wretched black stench of negative thoughts and stress. My cup overflows with warmth, love, and therapy as I let off steam. My coughing holds my world together because it is a quiet obsession that feeds my heart.

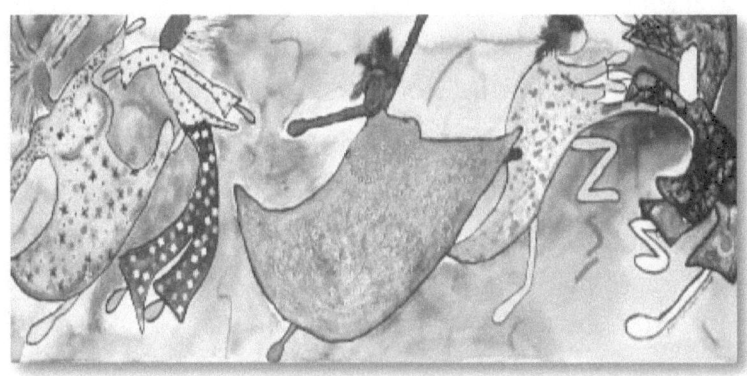

I'VE NEVER MADE A MISTAKE...

Cough into Your Own Cup

> *"The artist is a receptacle for emotions
> that come from all over the place:
> from the sky, from the earth, from a scrap of paper,
> from a passing shape, from a spider's web."*
>
> —Pablo Picasso

My creativity is my lifeline to the soul. It's like an IV drip that sustains and nourishes me through the illness called life.

Thoughts can rule you or you can rule them. Think about how you fill your mug: Is it half-filled with happy thoughts or half-empty with only negativity? Is it your cesspool or your hot tub?

We all have our own means of coping. You may drink, develop a sex addiction, be angry all the time, overeat, go postal, be a work-a-holic, or beat your canary. But channeling your energy constructively provides therapy, a means of survival.

Do something for you. Fill up that cup with Self-a-Steam. Don't be codependent; be self-dependent. Enjoy a cuppa creativity, exercise (it creates a natural high), get acupuncture (it's like poking holes to release all that pressure) or reflexology. Go to a counselor, get a massage, travel, volunteer. Be a mom, a business owner, a husband, or an employee. But most of all, be a donor to yourself.

Seriousness can be the death of our creative orgasms. That is why I try to live with a light mindset. My ideas are my sperm and Walt Disney's Cough is how I direct them. Be like a Danish donor and cough up something that will provide respite from the day-to-day by giving to yourself or giving to the world.

I wonder what Walt Disney's sperm looked like.

23

THE SOUND OF MUCUS

How to Escape the Phlegm in Your Life

"U*ghhhpheeh,*" I said, clearing my throat.

"What are you doing?" my friend Sheila asked.

"*Phleggggummmmm,*" I said. "I am trying to hack up my own self-pity. My sadness over my foam curlers stopping foaming has got viscosity. I am in the thick of my own self-producing *Waaaah-it-sucks-to-be-me* frolic!"

"Why don't you just stop your pity party?"

"Because it's my protective blanket!" I exclaimed. "It keeps me from drying out. It's like flypaper: It stops people from helping me."

"Oh, for pity's sake. Why don't you give up that kind of thinking for Lent?"

"I've tried, but it's as tenacious as skid marks on a toilet bowl. It's got me swimming in my own cesspit of distress because no one Repinned my Pinterest Pin of me trying to teach the monkeys at the zoo how to do the "see no evil, hear no evil, speak no evil" pose, using my rubber baby-hands finger puppets.

"Oh, pleeeease."

"Did you know I got only six hundred and forty-seven likes on my Facebook post of my gerbil doing the samba?" I cried. "I'm also lamenting getting in the wrong line at the grocery store. I spent multiple minutes assessing who would be the first to get through checkout. I was sure it was going to be the juvenile who was so skinny he had to tease his hair to keep his pants up. He was a walking Pepé Le Pew with the body odor of a marijuana budtender. His t-shirt looked like it had fought with a paper shredder and lost. His pants were posing as leg warmers. He begged to tell the world: "I have no money; this will just take a sec."

Sheila shook her head.

"I can't believe I totally misread him," I moaned. "He was buying a stick of gum and couldn't decide which flavor was his favorite!

"'I'll take a stick of spearmint, please,' he proudly declared after five minutes of hemming and hawing.

"'Oh, sugar, you don't want *thhhat*,' dripped the clerk. 'The "spear" in spearmint is dangerous. Why don't you try strawberry watermelon? The water in the watermelon will help hydrate you. You look as puckered as a prune in a suntanning bed.'

"'I have to avoid strawberries,' he demurred. 'I'm allergic to straw.'

"And then," I moaned, "it turns out he was paying with his monthly allowance, which he got in pennies, *aaaand* he had to return the Milky Way candy bar he had bought four years ago because it had dried out. How could I have been *sooooooo* wrong?" I whimpered.

"Oh, just go blow your nose," sighed Sheila.

I let that negative tune sing in my head. I had created my own Sound of Mucus when I could have heard the Sound of Music instead.

Von Trapp-ed

Mucus and wallowing in life's self-pity have a lot in common. They both have a mission: to reproduce. Too much is *not* a good thing. They both create antibodies that can work for or against you. And they can both leave you stuck in a sticky situation.

I aspire to be like the Von Trapp Family from *The Sound of Music*. They were always cheery and well-behaved, always doing the right thing. They escaped the unimaginable by singing their way through crises—thwarting danger while remaining well-dressed and pristine, their hair always in the right place. They must have had a great MANEtain Toolbox.

Before Eliza died, I struggled with day-to-day uncertainties. *Should I buy the embossed toilet paper or plain?* I faced each day as if I were climbing every mountain. Still, I tried to be like Julie Andrews. Little merry me, pouncing along the hillside, dancing in the rainbow-colored raindrops…it was actually sleet and snow, but

I'VE NEVER MADE A MISTAKE...

instead of being Debbie Downer, I thought positive by pretending it was sunshine and happiness. Looking over the hills, singing to my heart's content, I grabbed a tree and twirled like Maria. I soaked in the clouds, envisioning puffs of cotton candy. Then…as my hand skated around the bark…I got slivers in my palm and snow dropped on my head, encouraging my hair to 'fro out and my ears to evoke eggplants. In an instant, my Sound of Music had turned to the Sound of Mucus.

Or at least that's how it felt.

That was until life shifted out from under my feet like a level nine earthquake when my child died. White flakes, splinters, and Purple People Eater ears are really minor annoyances compared to life's major traumas.

Every time someone close to me died, I found it harder to be a Von Trapp, to be positive and light. I listened to self-help tapes, which reminded me to breathe deeply and utilize each breath. Unfortunately, what I inhaled smelled like a high school locker room. *Boy, my pits stink.*

So I focused inward, instructing myself to release my negative thoughts to the universe. When I sent my pity-party up to the higher powers, the response was "Recipient no longer at this number. No forwarding address."

The self-help tape also advised me to walk up the stairs toward the Pillar of Life. Unfortunately, I tripped and landed on the pet bed, which held our cat coughing up a furball and our incontinent dog tinkling a pee puddle.

What I did learn was to clean out that closet of knickknacks—the little stressors in life—to make room for a shovel, duct tape, goulashes, zipties, and all my favorite people to help me through the natural (and unnatural) disasters.

It's Snot Easy

Eventually you have to choose your battles—choose where you will expend your energy. Although I can't always be Maria, I can forge forward on the trails of life. In times of trouble, I draw on my creativity. I penned a message of hope.

Climb Every Mountain

Life is like climbing a mountain.
Sometimes the journey is steep and difficult.
At times one knows not the hardships ahead
nor what lies around the bend.
Progress can be slow and troublesome.
It may require stopping, stepping back,
and changing direction.
It is the challenges of this journey
that increase our knowledge and strength.
We grow wiser with each step we take.
We learn that the limits in front of us are but illusions,
to be challenged and conquered with our own inner strength
and our belief that there are no limits.
It is in our ability to see that beauty exists
within each challenge and hardship.
Surrounding us are more positives than failures
and more growth than limits.
Progress may be slow but progress is there.
The support of others along the journey
is the rope that offers us confidence and direction.
We continue moving forward,
obtaining our goals, fulfilling our dreams.

> *We curse not at the rock that offers little footing;*
> *we hold no bitterness towards the wall*
> *that is steep and narrow!*
> *We accept them for what they are*
> *and understand the uniqueness of each stone and crevice.*
> *We forge on, believing in the specialness of all challenges*
> *and in our own abilities to overcome those challenges*
> *to reach the peak, the Peak of Life.*

As I read this poem at Eliza's mountain-park memorial, the snow clung to me like a two-year-old about to be taken by force from her mother. The cold penetrated my soul like icicles crawling under my skin. A silent demon beckoned me to give in to my pain and sorrow. I didn't want to forge on. I wanted to let go of the rope that steadied me and urged me forward. It seemed easier than facing another deep, dark crevice. As I looked around, the world seemed to be blanketed in jagged stones and cold, unforgiving walls of torment.

The river adjacent to where we all gathered, which I imagined to be like my unleashed tears, was frozen. This provided me a brief respite in the form of a small wave of laughter. We had brought a rose to throw into the stream to signify Eliza's moving on. But a frosty sheet of ice acts as a platter—not a waiter carrying that platter. The rose simply sat on the skating rink–like surface.

Upon my return to the park the next day, I found the rose was gone. I am sure an animal was a steward of Eliza's continued journey.

One Flush Away

The presence of loved ones willing to brave the three-below temperatures to bid farewell to a little girl they would never meet tapped me on the brain. It pleaded with me to keep grasping for my next breath, which begged to surrender to the chokehold of those Gollum-like fingers of loss. Pine trees towered over us in their statuesque stance as though with a message: *We are here to protect you.* The mountains in the distance reminded me of their hardiness. Although their silhouette had shifted and crumbled under the forces of nature, they epitomized resilience. And their beauty was enhanced by all they had withstood.

Mother Nature had taken from me, but she was also generous. My pain and loss were what I needed to keep moving toward the Peak of Life. What I could not do was stop and swim in my despair. I needed to focus on the gifts of my husband, my son, and the wealth of love enriching my life.

If, like the Van Trapp family, you have to worry about being shot or escaping from one country to the next, it's natural to choke a bit on your own self-phlegm. But don't indulge in wallowing too long or you might be captured.

If your concern is whether your toilet paper roll should pull from the top or the bottom, you might want to hack up that loogie and flush it down the toilet. There is only so much room in that body of yours for the Sound of Mucus.

24
PARACHUTING WITH A PURPOSE

"If at first you don't succeed... skydiving may not be for you!"

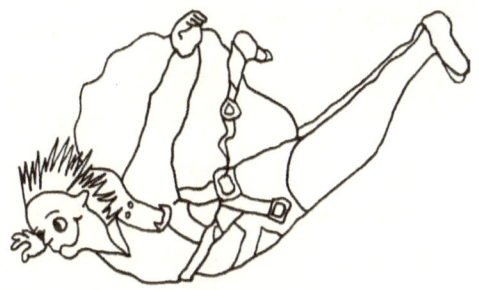

Planning your own death is hard. I know, 'cause I've tried.

I considered skydiving without a parachute—or conveniently forgetting to open it right before I hit the ground. But in the United States, you must jump with a certified instructor at least seven times before being allowed out on your own; that's a lot of time and effort put into a skill you never plan to use!

I'd need to go to a country that would support my cause.

Unfortunately, I can't find any tourist websites or brochures touting: "The fun, perfect place to end it all."

I know I can't go to Uganda—at least not to drown myself. I rafted the Nile there, and their safety precautions were stricter than gate security at a Def Leopard concert.

Geez, it shouldn't be this much work to end my life!

Bye-Bye, Beni

Have you visited a third world country lately to bite the bullet and kick the bucket? Be aware that they are hip to travelers' safety. Mainly because they are beseiged by foreigners plopping their too-heavy-to-fly-for-free suitcases on their doorstep under the guise of "I am here to save you, fellow humans," when, in fact, they are about to go out the back door and get bitten by a boa constrictor,

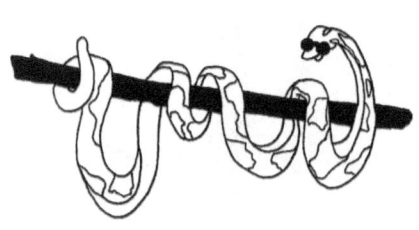

or raft through rapids whose house-sized vortexes toss them around like a washing machine overloaded with towels. It brings new meaning to the mantra "Just keep spinning." Isn't that how it goes?

You might try swimming in the Beni River in North Bolivia, which is filled with deadly piranhas. It also boasts pink dolphins, which are endearing, but so ugly they might be able to scare you to death! (Whilst swimming in just such river, a pink dolphin rubbed against my leg and I jumped into our boat faster than a wild gorilla chews on coca leaves.)

Now, you may be wondering: Why are these thoughts spiraling around in my head?

While caring for my mother, I conceived a plan that if I got Alzheimer's or any other terminal illness, I would find a way to protect others from watching the disease ravage my body and brain. I didn't want *them* having to write stories of pain and perseverance, this time with the focus on me:

> "*Tick by tick, the clock robs you of your dignity, your confidence, your ability to eat, breath, walk, and think on your own. Tick by tick, it sucks away the strength of the person who is caring for you, along with their friends and family, robbing them of their ability to handle all the Crimes Against Their Sanity.*"

Caregiving is often a no-win situation. When those wanting a say in the matter have no intention of helping fix what's the matter, it makes you madder than a hatter!

In May of 2013, *National Geographic's* cover featured a photo of a baby with the title: "This Baby Will Live to 120." While on the surface that sounds well and good, I hope that baby does not develop a crippling disease or major aging issues, because as my grandmother who lived to be ninety-six proclaimed: "It isn't worth it."

Unless there are more ways to provide support for family and caregivers—financially, emotionally, and legally—then that baby may live to be a hundred twenty, but everyone around him will sink holding up the boat that's keeping him afloat. And if he's adrift on his own, then what?

Just Keep Swimming

Third world countries are not your luxury trips to suicide. The time I rafted down the Nile in Uganda, I learned that if you fall out of the raft, within seconds you have some sweet-looking kayaker saving your white Mzungu booty (which one rafting guide complained blinded him—Ugandan rafters wear sunglasses for that reason!). They are not letting you go down on their watch. It's bad for tourism.

I'VE NEVER MADE A MISTAKE...

While swimming in the *Rio Beni,* my guide had a "do not eat my tourist" stick, which he beat against the water to dissuade the piranhas from feasting on my juicy, juicy mangos. He also had a giant handheld blender that he lowered about six feet down and then spun around to whirl away the creatures, all the while chanting: "Not this one, dear piranhas; not this one." The pink dolphins dug the swirling, so they stuck around for the fun.

If you want to avoid returning home with excess baggage, I'm sure you could pay your guide extra to halt the anit-piranha swirl.

One Trumped-Up Jump and Four Parachutes

The United States makes it even harder to stop breathing. When my son Bob was eighteen, he flew from Colorado to Vermont via New York. His connecting flight got delayed for twenty-two hours, so he spent the night on JFK's luxury indoor/outdoor carpet.

At 10:34 p.m., he called me. "I'm hungry," he said.

"Go buy some food," I encouraged. "On us."

At 11:12 p.m., the phone rang.

"This is the Port Authority Police!" a gruff voice yelled. "Is your son on any drugs? Is he mentally stable?"

"Why do you ask?" I yelped, unsure how to respond. When was a teenager ever mentally stable?

"We just caught him sitting on a tenth-story parking garage ledge, eating a sandwich. Why would he do that?"

"He was hungry?" I ventured.

"What was he thinking?!"

"I never know what he's thinking," I replied. "His brain won't be fully developed 'til he's twenty-five. Wait seven years and I'll ask him then."

"Why would he sit on a ledge that high?"

I searched for an answer that would get this stranger to stop screaming at me and let me talk to my son. "He lives in Colorado and he's a rock climber and an extreme skier, so he's not afraid of heights?"

"He's an idiot."

"Thank you," I replied. "I'll tell his father. We can debate whom he takes after."

Click! went the other end of the line.

A hair-raising thirty minutes later, Bob called.

"Mom, I went to the top of this parking garage to enjoy the view while I ate. After about ten minutes, I looked down and saw eight cop cars and an ambulance way below me. I wondered what was going on, so I hopped down and skateboarded to the elevator. Two cops jumped out, grabbed me, and handcuffed me.

"'What are you doing? What are you doing?' they kept yelling at me.

"'I was hungry?' I answered."

He gets that deductive reasoning from me.

"What were *they* thinking?!" I belted out.

"They thought I wanted to jump."

"Was your sandwich that bad?"

"They searched my bag three times."

"You'll never eat *there* again."

"I'm going to my indoor/outdoor carpeting. I'm beat."

At 1:00 a.m., the phone rang.

"*Moooooooooom*, I don't know why I'm calling you about this, but I've lost my wallet. When they searched my bag, they didn't close the zipper. I had two hundred dollars in there, *Mooooooooooom*!! And I can't get back into my gate because I don't have my ID."

"I'll figure this out—don't panic," I said as I panicked.

I called the airline three times. Bob asked the gate agent if he could talk to me, but she said that was against regulations. And calling the Port Authority Police certainly wouldn't be helpful—they were the ones who had created this mess!

I called at least ten different phone numbers. Finally I got a woman whom I now refer to as one of my many parachutes in life. She was the paging operator for the airport's white courtesy phones, and she turned out to be an angel.

She got Bob a seat flying out at 8:00 a.m. rather than at five p.m. that evening. I stayed on hold with her for two hours, which is the time it took for her to find someone to help get Bob into his gate area, report Bob's missing wallet to the police, and get an attendant to retrieve his passport out of his checked bag. She updated me at every opportunity, and updated Bob.

"Thank you for helping us out so much," I told her.

"If that were my son, I would want someone to do the same," she replied.

In the end, Bob got on that morning flight and met his Aunt Edna and Uncle Don in Vermont.

At 11:00 a.m., I got another call.

"This is your insurance company. Do you have a son named Bob?"

"YES!!!!" I replied, even more panicked than before. There was a lot of panicking going on in these twenty-four hours.

"I have a woman on the line who says she found your son's wallet."

I exhaled in relief. "Thank you. Thank you so much."

"If this were my child, I would want someone to do the same for me. I'll put you through to her."

The agent was my second parachute of the day—the very, very long day.

"My husband found your son's wallet by a bus stop on his way home from his night shift," a frail voice told me. "It doesn't have any money in it, but it has his credit cards and ID. I couldn't find his phone number anywhere, so I called the number on his insurance card."

"Thank you sooooo much," I gushed.

"If this was our grandson, we would want somebody to help him out."

They were our third and fourth parachutes—people who saved us from our fall.

The woman mailed Bob's wallet to him in Vermont. I sent both her and the airport paging operator gifts made by the women in Uganda.

The Port Authority Police called and apologized, explaining that they'd dealt with two suicides in the past month and were jumpy. They also explained that they are required by law to handcuff anyone whose mental status is in question, in order to protect themselves and others from getting hurt.

Embracing the Rip Cord

I don't really want to kill myself if I get a terminal illness. At least that's my thought now, while I am healthy and strong. But I did tell my family I wouldn't want to suffer like my mother did. I also told my children that if they were fighting because of me, they should put me in a nursing home. That I wouldn't want their relationship to suffer under the strain of caring for me, especially because I wouldn't be around to put them in timeout for fighting. They reserved me a room at Sunny Manor that day.

If, like me, you get the urge to take a skydive without the parachute, stop and take a step back. Get off that plane and go for a walk. Swim with the dolphins or treat yourself to a sandwich on the Empire State Building (which *does* have guardrails!). Things may not have changed when you return from your break, but *you* will have.

Instead of looking at skydiving as an opportunity to *not* pull the rip cord, look at your parachute as a resource for when your plane is going down. Don't be afraid to ask for help, express your weaknesses, or reach out to people—if only for the reason that something doesn't feel right.

Parachute in tandem.

Find hope in the unexpected person. That parachute could be the airline's paging operator or a grandma you'll never meet.

No matter how big the waves, how hungry the piranhas, or how high the lows, you have the hot kayakers there to save your beautiful Mzungu ass when it's going down, Bolivians to beat off the piranhas, and Port Authority cops to catch your fall so they can handcuff you.

If you find yourself sinking instead of swimming, take a leap of faith. For now, I'm gonna *just keep spinning* in my freefall, but eventually I'll pull the rip cord that will keep me safe.

25

SAVE A HORSE, RIDE A COWBOY

Your Attitude Determines Your Ride

Sex is like doing laundry: it's a cycle.

It happens maybe once a week—and if not, when you are desperate.

Things get turned on, turned off.

Accidental shrinkage can occur.

Other times, wet, hot, and bothered is the theme.

Frequent cold rinses are required.

I'VE NEVER MADE A MISTAKE...

Someone or something may get hung out to dry.

Then there's the rinse and repeat.

What's left is drained.

Marriage is a like your wardrobe. It starts out crisp, colorful, and full of possibilities, but after years of wear and tear, it can become dull, faded, and lifeless…unless, of course, you mix up your loads.

You know, that sex cycle: Add some "fluff and tumble." If it becomes delicate and degrades with time, dry clean it. It'll stiffen up in a good way. Or try sink-washing—you'll like that labor-intensive hand work. *Is that your laundry or are you just happy to see me?*

Most of us try to keep our marriages fresh, tidy, and vibrant.

We try not to fold when things get tough.

Pain and Torture Can Be Fun

My husband and I make sure to spend quality time as a couple. In fact, we enjoy a weekly "date night": going to physical therapy together. Sometimes we even enjoy being manipulated twice a week.

At PT, we get to share our problems, including but not limited to what body parts hurt or why I'm not happy with him for refusing to share the ThighMaster and the toys. Oh, the toys.

Our "sex" toys include exercise "Thera-Bands," which come in as many colors as condoms, and the Thera-Band ball, which offers all sorts of unique positions. We get aroused when the strength in our weary joints increases by more than five percent over the previous week.

Of course, at PT, sex is limited. But when isn't it? At home, we have our own monogrammed foam rollers and therapy balls. Can lovemaking count as my required PT? Instead of whips and chains, we can use glow-in-the-dark Thera-bands.

Sweating It Out

Allen and I iron out the wrinkles in our marriage by accepting our differences and by communicating.

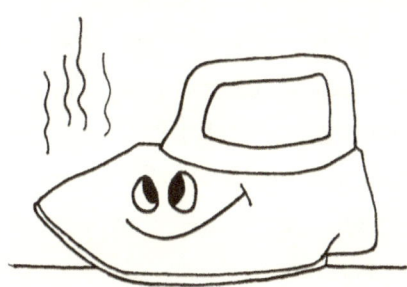

We take our wedding vows seriously: "I promise to be true to you in good times and in bad, in sickness and in health." Of course, if Allen had his way, the sickness and health part would have contained a clause excluding night sweats.

"Honey, honey!" I yelled. "Look: a special TV episode featuring night sweats! You have to watch it with me—*pleeeeeasssse.*"

Looking at me as though I had suggested removing him from life support, he asked, "Why would I want to do that? I have my own live show every night."

"Honey, it's on *The Tonight Show Starring Jimmy Fallon;* it can't be that bad. I am ecstatic that we sufferers are finally getting due attention to our misery."

I plopped in front of the television naked (to keep my body temp down), hoping to learn all about these hot flashes that have ruled my life, compelling me to give up wearing anything inside the house but aluminum foil. When my furnace flares, I can cook dinner on it.

"I just want to see if there is some way to control my nuclear reactor," I sighed.

"Why would you want to do that?" replied Allen. "It's all the passion and intensity we have left in our marriage."

I stared at him. "Sweetheart, it's not really a turn-on that you can save money on the heating bill every time I have a hot flash more explosive than an interview with Stormy Daniels."

"It is to me!" Allen smiled gleefully. "I don't even need to own a barbecue grill. When your heat's at full throttle, I'm just a hot dog away from being satiated."

Jimmy Fallon let me down. It turns out what had promised to be the end-all answer to my chronic problem was the sizzling new band Nathaniel Rateliff & The Night Sweats, singing my new favorite theme song, "S.O.B." I'm sure the song is about actual night sweats; it's gotta be. Wait—maybe it's about marriage. Son of a bitch!

"Self-Entertainment"

Allen wanted to take me to Lowes for our thirtieth wedding anniversary. At first I fought it. I mean, at least take me to Walmart, where creepy men in the parking lot tell me they like my "TT." (How was I to know the model of our Audi rental car?!) Or to the appliance store, where we can further explore the rinse-and-repeat cycle.

Embracing the give-and-take approach to our relationship, I followed my husband into Lowes. Stepping up to the service desk, he announced to a crowd of spectators: "I'm the guy with the caulk."

I refrained from wetting my pants and wheezing as I held in my response. *Hey, everyone—he's the guy with the "caulk"!* I wanted to shout. *And, boy, does it do the laundry well!*

Allen hadn't mentioned that he had caulk on hold at the service desk, and no one else seemed to notice the pun.

Maybe that's why he calls me "self-entertaining."

Marriage Can Be a Rush

True love is following your husband to the ends of the earth—or to a Rush Limbaugh concert. My friend Trudy followed her husband, Todd.

"You didn't!" I stammered. "How could you? This can't be true."

"I am afraid so," she told me. "It was a warm summer night at Red Rocks, and we were excited to be at the beautiful outdoor amphitheater. We were searched by security at the entrance, along with all the heavy-metal-looking fans."

"Shouldn't that have been your first clue?"

"I thought it was the next generation of Rush Limbaugh supporters."

"What did Todd think?"

"He thought he'd better keep an eye on his wallet."

"Weren't you worried?"

"Yes, but only for those poor boys who couldn't see past their curtains of hair. We also fretted about the rancid skunk smell."

"I think that was pot."

"Really? Anyway, we started getting *really* suspicious when chords from a bass guitar reverberated off the rocks around us. But then we were encouraged when a munchkin-like voice started singing 'Working Man.'"

"Why would Rush Limbaugh have a band?" I questioned.

"I asked Todd that very same thing," Trudy replied. "I said, 'Honey, why would these boys who look like girls want to hear this music that makes my nose hairs curl? Don't you think Rush would be a little put out? I bet these boys don't even practice safe sex.'

"'Maybe Rush is trying to attract a more diverse crowd' was Todd's reply.

"Then Todd looked at the tickets again. In big bold letters, they read: *RUSH*. He had bought tickets for the rock band Rush."

The moral of this story? Love has no boundaries—and, in this case, no brains…which is sometimes the strongest bond for marriage.

It's All in the Wrist—or in This Case, the Reins

"I feel like I'm riding a horse," I moaned.

"What do you mean riding a horse?" Allen yawned as he turned his back to me to sleep.

"Our marriage is either plodding along and comfortable, or—*BAM!*—we have to hold on to the reins for dear life."

"Honey," he said, "you chose to climb into the saddle; you should have been ready to ride."

"Chose to climb into the saddle???" I sputtered. "I think I tripped and fell in the water trough. Besides, I didn't know there would be so many hurdles."

"Dear, that is because you let those brambles get under your britches. You gotta not let life get your giddy-up so often."

"But, dear," I whinnied, "don't you ever want more?"

"What more would I want?" he asked. "I have you."

I shook my head.

"Honey," I said, "I think they let you out of the wrong gate and maybe it's time to put you out to pasture."

"That's fine," he murmured. "But can you do it after I sleep?"

Marriage is like riding a horse:

- You might get bucked.
- Sometimes you want to bolt.
- "Tack" is helpful for communicating.
- You must hold on to the reins, but not too tightly.
- You've got to love your cowboy or cowgirl for who he or she is (goose rump and all).
- Your attitude determines your ride.

May the horse be with you. I think I'll go do the laundry.

26
TWITCH, TWITCH— I CAN'T STOP THIS TWITCH

Can't They Let Sleeping Dogs Lie?

I fret and brood so much they call me Twitch.

I worry about the toaster oven electrocuting me.

The heebie-jeebies overtake me when Lisa Jean's oxygen tank is turned on—what if it shocks my silky hair right out of its pores? And I fear for both our lives when the tank shuts off accidently; does that mean I'll have to breathe for her? That might keep me from my nap.

The basement bathroom is my only sanctuary from the dishwasher blaring that the dishes are clean—and who cares, anyway? And just whose idea was it to have the phone's Bluetooth *and* the clothes washer both let out blood-curdling screams when turned on?

Finally, I won't—absolutely won't—get into the Audi. You have no idea how much Audis beep.

A Dogged Dilemma

I hate the medication they give me to help me with my jitters—I have anxiety over anxiety pills. I have tried to take them willingly, but my mind and teeth won't cooperate. I pick up a mouthful of food, drop it on the floor, and then, although the pill is buried in peanut butter, I eat around it. Talented, I know. It's like I'm a dog chasing my own tail. I do that sometimes, too.

My trauma stems from childhood, inflicted on me by my family, all with good intentions. (Since I can't blame the dog, I might as well blame my owners!) It was those darn invisible electric fences: Now I'm afraid of every high-pitched sound emitted from any electronic device.

I may be a lovable lab, but I have feelings, too. And clearly worries. Lots of worries.

But my parents, Allen and Joan, they've been good to me. I'm twelve now, and in dog years that's old—very, very old. And overall, I turned out pretty well. I've never done drugs—not even my prescribed ones—or failed in school or taken the car without permission.

Allen and Joan have always tried to do what's best for me. But when I was a pup, they were new to this parenthood thing—and it's a big responsibility. Juggling this new cute-but-loud demanding ball of energy with their careers and lives took them a while to figure

Twitch, Twitch—I Can't Stop This Twitch

out. As they tried to establish a new normal at home, they were inundated with opinions and ideas from every side.

I have watched my reasons-for-living tread the same course with their human children. Over the years, while curled up at their feet, I've observed them read "how to" books, watch videos, and surf the Web, overwhelmed with choices and bombarded with conflicting information.

It makes me want to chew off my own ear.

Babies and Teenagers Are Not Returnable

It started with their newborn. They sought to understand how to train it to sleep and how to interpret its five different cries, just as they had tried to understand my five different barks. To me, it seems obvious that children and I have the same basic needs when we bark or cry: (1) we are hungry, (2) we have to pee or just did, (3) we are in pain, (4) pay attention to us, or (5) we are tired and we'd like a beer. Wait—that's me, not the kid. The kid didn't seek out beer 'til he was sixteen.

User manuals are not a one-size-fits-all. Children and puppies do not play by the rules. This became increasingly apparent as I listened to Allen discuss parenthood with his friend, Jeff, both of them twistedly twitching over their tribulations. I could never decide whose twitch was twitchier.

Allen and Joan's son was six months old and Jeff's son, Carl, was just over eight months. Here's how the conversation went:

"There are countless parenting experts with advice on things like sleep training, eating, et cetera," Jeff sighed, "but the information is overwhelming and inevitably contradictory. I've read all these books and I'm still baffled."

"I hear you," said Allen. "Figuring out children leaves me more confused than when Joan tells me I'm not romantic enough—I mean, I thought every woman would love a wheelbarrow for an anniversary gift.

"I was not prepared for the weight of responsibility of having cherubs," Allen went on. "Do you think we can return them?"

"Nah, we'd never get all our money back," Jeff quipped.

"Then what do we do?" Allen pleaded.

"My parents had nine kids," Jeff said. "They knew they would finally get it right with one of them. At least we don't have a litter of babies. And this can't be harder than raising a puppy, can it? What do *you* think, Twitch?"

I know I'm a dog, but I'm not just any ol' dog. This dog has been around the block and to the dog park and back. I may not have been able to respond, but I sure as heck had the answers. My bark is smarter than my bite; too bad they can't understand what I'm saying. If they could, I would tell them:

1. Babies and teenagers are non-returnable. But it is okay, when sleep-deprived, to call your son Cooper even if his name is Carl.

2. Babies and teenagers eat a lot and sleep a lot. And although you don't have to burp a teenager, you'll see the same amount of spit-up.

3. Relax. *D.O.T., D.O.T., D.O.T.: Don't Over Think.* If you build the foundation and give your child the right tools, they will be able to withstand almost anything.

4. The experts learned just like you: through trial and error. Allow yourself mistakes, don't put yourself on the chopping block, and don't let others court-martial you with their judgments.

Only Dogs Can Walk on Water

I hung out in the kitchen one day as Mom prepared my gourmet concoction of dried dog food, peanut butter, and the medication I always find hidden in the peanut butter.

"I feel so guilty," Joan sighed. "What if I'm messing up my kids? What if I'm not doing enough? I'm always comparing myself to others; it's impossible not to."

She confides in me when she thinks I'm not listening. But I am all ears and I keep her secrets.

Frustrated, I barked twice, telling her: *Listen up: I have hung out at the Joneses' house and their Christmas newsletter is embellished upon. Little Junior did not start walking on water when he was two—he was actually four. Guilt is something you inflict upon yourself. Be like me: I live virtually guilt-free—except when I sneak a treat or two. Ahhh, heaven.*

Bark after bark, I encouraged:

- *Maintain perspective (and patience), whether your two-legged baby is small or big. The world is huge and your child is just trying to figure it all out.*

- *It is easy to get frustrated or angry at the tantrums or pushback or lack of understanding. Try to be empathetic.*

- *For example, I was very patient with YOU when you didn't like that I peed on your neighbor at the Mommy and Me playgroup. Well, I tell you, I wasn't the only one there who deserved the title of "bitch"; that woman was judging you and your children. But her bark was worse than her bite. I showed her: My peeing got you to change groups.*

- *Stay calm and carry on. I took deep breaths when Allen threw a hissy fit when I crawled onto the couch with muddy paws. I have*

I'VE NEVER MADE A MISTAKE...

to be patient with him; he hasn't figured out yet that a hard wood floor does not qualify as comfy.

- Toddlers, teenagers, and puppies have a lot in common: They have an abundance of uncontrolled energy, they drool, they "do" before they think, and they give you tests you are sure to flunk.

- Carry around a photo of your teenager from when they were two. This will remind you that the temper tantrums will abate, just as they did at age seven.

- Avoid biting when a growl will do.

A Baby, a Bucket, and a Goat

I wish we could all be as lucky as my owners, able to travel the world, volunteering. They've learned so much by witnessing how others live. It has helped them let go of their own expectations formed by society's norms.

They got to see firsthand Alejandra, a one-year-old in Bolivia, content and smiling as she sat in the dirt with a only a bug to play with.

In El Salvador, they delighted in Julio's joy when he found out what he looked like. Joan was reading her interactive children's book, *Peek-A-Boo Who?*, which has a mirror on the final page, to a classroom of six-year-olds. Julio was beside himself as he viewed his reflection for the very first time.

Serving with Outreach Uganda, they befriended a teenager named Apwonyo Betty and discovered that, like any teenager around the world, she wanted autonomy from her parents. When their organization provided the opportunity for women and girls to make products to sell in the U.S., Apwonyo Betty and her peers were intent upon producing something different from their mothers. So

Twitch, Twitch—I Can't Stop This Twitch

instead of the jewelry their moms created out of poster paper, they crafted beaded bracelets out of wood.

My family discovered that teenagers in Japan are called "teenage sushi" because they roll their eyes a lot.

I can't travel with my family, so I watch TV. One of my favorite movies, *Babies*, exemplifies ways to put your mind at ease as a parent. With so many choices, consumerism can be overwhelming. This brilliant documentary demonstrates that your child needs far less than you feel you need to give her. The story documents two babies from rural areas—one from Namibia, the other from Mongolia—and two from urban areas: Japan and the United States. My favorite scene is when Bayar from Mongolia is taking a bath in a metal bucket and a goat comes and drinks the bath water. No fuss, no muss—everybody's happy. I bet that goat likes belly rubs, too.

No matter what method you use, it's important to see how others live. Watching others subsist more basically helps you stay in the present, appreciating each day and not getting ahead of yourself about when your child will achieve his or her next milestone. A baby, a bucket, and a goat remind you to keep it simple and lower your expectations.

My parents are still trying to convince me to pee outside the house. I hate to break it to them, but this is one milestone I might not get on board with.

Enjoy Some Dog Days

Sometimes it's okay to not have GAS: to not Give A Shit. Joan had a bad case of GAS raising children, especially while they were in school. She was like a member of the cracker jack brigade on a pachyderm parade in *The Jungle Book*.

Joan was marching along through life with all the other elephants (the mothers at Anna's preschool) when—"Company, HALT!"—a volunteer was needed to organize the Silly Putty by color. It also happened that someone was needed to differentiate the Silly Putty from what was either moldy food, throw-up, or little Johnny's vegan lunch. Joan was an elephant with a tiny backbone. When it came to saying no, she was just one big dorsal bump.

Imagine Colonel Hathi, the lead elephant of the Jungle Patrol (and a "pompous old wind bag," according to his wife, Winifred), as the teacher of the pint-size preschoolers. He lines up his marching mammal mommas by bugling: "Company, left FACE! Volunteers for a special mission will step one pace forward." All the other elephants in the long row facing him take one step back, leaving Joan as the lone volunteer.

In reality, there was no family *Elephantidae*. Just Joan and her need to please.

Even now, at age seventeen, Anna lectures Joan: "You have to get over the need to 'step up to the plate' for everything."

I say, let sleeping dogs lie and don't try to please everyone. Don't always come when you are called. I know it's not always clear how to give to oneself while managing children, a career, and a spouse, but take that leash off your neck, cut yourself some slack, choose your battles, and let the rest go. Seek help from those around you. Take yourself for a walk to get some exercise. Plan date nights when you and your mate can chase a ball for entertainment; it's amazingly brain-numbing. Take puppy uppers not doggie downers. Think positive and avoid getting bad GAS. Take it from me: I'm a perfect role model and I don't volunteer for anything.

Beware: A Dog Can't Hold Its Licker

Man, that hamburger smelled good! Freshly grilled and sitting there on the table just out of my reach. I was twitching with my urge to steal it. Now that I'm older, all I want to eat is meat. But I knew it wasn't for me, even though I'd been invited to this cookout.

"Boy, oh boy," Jeff sighed. "Did I learn a big lesson today."

"What's that?" Allen asked.

"Now that Carl is fifteen, I have to let go and trust him more," Jeff responded.

"Why?" asked Allen.

"Well, for one thing, he's smarter than me!" Jeff laughed. "Plus, I can't control everything."

"Could you ever control everything?" Allen replied. "I sure couldn't."

"Probably not, but even less now."

"What happened?"

"It all started when I found a small clear container with something hard, jagged, and gold-colored in the driver's seat of the car," Jeff explained. "I was sure it was Carl's and I was sure it was drugs. I panicked and I called the juvenile detention center."

As an outsider listening in, I thought Jeff's reaction was a little ruff. I quickly reminded myself how dog-tired he was from all of Carl's restless rompings.

"'Douglas County Juvenile Hotline,' said the voice on the other end. 'How can I help?'

"'I found this vial in our car shortly after teaching my son how to drive. I think it fell out of his pocket. I can't tell what it is and I'm concerned it could be drugs.'

"The teenage expert puffed up like a peacock and told me, 'Teenagers are like magicians. They want you to watch the left hand while the right hand is doing the deceiving. Drugs are disguised in all different ways. Drug dealers can take a piece of paper the size of a dot and turn it into a Quaalude. You can't take any chances. Take the vial to the police station and have it examined.'"

Jeff sighed heavily before continuing his story.

"When I got there, the cop laughed," he said. "'I think it's spray paint,' he told me.

"Still, driving him to school the next day, I confronted Carl. 'Is this yours?' I asked.

"'No, it's not mine. What is it?'

"And that's when Julia in the back seat perked up and said, 'That's mine! I went gold-panning with the Gabels.'"

Jeff groaned. "I'm too old for this."

I say, licker or drugs, telling the truth or lying, a point will come when that tracking phone app can be disabled by your teenager and you won't even know it. Or when that small yellow hunk in that vial will be something you can't identify. You must learn to trust your teenager and hope he can control his licker and a lot of other things in his life.

Barking Up the Wrong Tree

Barking up the wrong tree is a recurring problem of mine. What really irks me is when I lose the squirrel I was chasing in the first place because it runs up another tree I'm *not* looking at. Much like my masters, I often waste time on problems that aren't

Twitch, Twitch—I Can't Stop This Twitch

really problems. (Okay, a squirrel *is* a problem, but I create a bigger problem by barking up the wrong tree!)

I say, GARP: Get A Real Problem—or at least learn to identify what is a true difficulty. I overheard this acronym from a friend of Joan's, Monique, who was confiding about her young son who had cancer. Monique said she and her husband came up with this by learning to ask themselves: "On a scale of zero to ten, how much energy do we want to expend?"

When something bad happens, one discovers that the little annoyances in life just don't matter anymore. Take the mother of the son born in a boy's body who has always known he is a girl, or the family of four with the six-year-old daughter who is diabetic, gluten-free, and dairy-free. Remember "The Sound of Mucus": Hack up your self-pity and spit it out. Prioritize your focus where it counts. If you are traversing the issue of whether your child is transgender, you may want to let it go that his or her room is not clean. Ask yourself: Is it disrespectful that the room is not clean, or is your child asserting his power in a world where he has little control?

If your son is doing well in school, you might not hound him for spilling his soda, eating that extra cookie, or failing to say "thank you" to everyone.

Joan said it well when her oldest graduated from college: "I shape-shift as my children shape-shift with age. Looking back on all the shit I sifted through to survive the shit storms, I see that some of what I worried over I didn't need to give a shit about."

Canine Words of Wisdom

- *Toxic Sock Syndrome is what happens when your teenager doesn't change her socks for days.*
- *Your child will be going "through a stage" until he is ninety.*

I'VE NEVER MADE A MISTAKE...

- *"How could you?" will be the most-uttered phrase by your child from middle school on, be it because you wore bike shorts in front of her friends, said hello, or breathed.*
- *"Rage with me" is all your teenager wants you to do when she's complaining. You don't need to fix things; you need to rage or let her rage.*
- *If your child can tell his math teacher that his test is stupid, he can order a pizza.*
- *Teenagers are often to parents as Mars is to an astronaut: No matter how much you push and probe, you'll find no signs of life.*
- *There's a reason God made white paint: so you can paint over the colors you don't like and start fresh. You can't start over with your kids, but you can paint over some of the problems and move on.*
- *Children are the reason I don't have children.*

Twitch is my name because of stress, strain, and allergies. When I was young, I used to stand on all fours and try to scratch my face with my hind leg…I'd fall flat on my furry rolls of puppy face fat. Now that I'm in my prime, I think I've done a pretty good job of training my masters to choose their battles.

Twitch, twitch, you are never going to stop your twitch. But you can control it. Stay away from things that can burn you, like the toaster oven. Avoid barking at the dishwasher, or your problem will linger long after the beep.

Be the person your dog thinks you are.

27

LAST DANCE

Lisa Jean: The Perfect Storm

*"Life isn't about waiting for the storm to pass.
It's about learning to dance in the rain."*

—Vivian Greene

My dance partner knows how to lead. Her four-foot-three-inch frame guides me with her wit, humor, charm, and authority. She is the center point of balance, as I and others follow her chassê through life.

I'VE NEVER MADE A MISTAKE...

My partner is Lisa Jean. The day Lisa twirled into our world in November of 1966 was the day life became a daily hoedown; shindigs galore became the norm. True, there were doctors, occupational therapists, and speech therapists. There were temper tantrums the size of Texas. There was sign language. There was also love and laughter—lots and lots of both.

For the first year of L.J.'s life, our parents didn't tell us, her seven siblings, that she had Down syndrome. They didn't want her to be treated any differently by the family. Our home was a three-ring circus and she fit right into the pandemonium. In fact, L.J. became the ringmaster: entertaining, spectacular, commanding, and another source of silliness. I remember that the singing of "This Old Man" around the dinner table just got louder as Lisa Jean joined in with her own version of the "knick-knack paddy-wack" chorus. She adapted to the hustle-bustle as much as we adapted to her.

Growing Up Gracefully

Even at age four, Lisa had a very definite purpose in this perplexing world. When her brothers Derrick and Matt went off to fight in Vietnam, she waved good-bye like the rest of us. But her heart didn't weigh as heavy because she didn't understand the complications of life. Matt was killed in 1971, shortly before Lisa was to begin kindergarten. A memorial fund was created in his name to raise money for a bus for Lisa's school, "First Creek," which served those with special challenges.

Lisa Jean was one of the first students with Down syndrome to graduate from high school in Colorado. She even went to Denver University. (My brother always said she was the smartest in the family because none of *us* could have gotten into DU!) She attended a special program on living skills. I know she taught the folks at DU a thing or two, too.

She moved out and had a roommate. The pair lived a bit like *Sesame Street's* Bert and Ernie, never aging and oftentimes thinking like seven-year-olds. Lisa eventually got a place of her own when her roommate wasn't happy about Lisa's putting her Rockin' Robin musical doll in the dumpster.

Lisa had many vocations. She was the star box-folder and bread-butterer at a pizza joint, a hostess with the mostest ticket collector at the movie theater, and a mischievous book organizer at a thrift store. Then, as she put it, she "retired." Instigated by a misunderstanding involving OCD–meets–paper products stolen from the bathroom and people's purses.

Silly and Sorry

> *"For the tiny amount of physical space*
> *she occupies in this world,*
> *she sure manages to take hold of and occupy*
> *an enormous amount of heart space in those she encounters."*
>
> —Mindy Vankalsbeek

Lisa has a way with words—very few words. Our brother Mark knows he is hot because Lisa is his number one fan.

"Hi, Big Butt!" Lisa says to him every time he enters the room.

"Aflac!" she muses.

"Can I give you a hug, Your Highness?" she asks anyone and everyone.

Confusion and chaos take the lead when she giggles and says "You're not my type, Stinky."

Idolized we feel, even though her endearment has eyes for all willing to feed her Diet Dr. Pepper addiction. She'll bop with the fireman at the grocery store, rumba with Michael Franti, cha-cha with J Bowman, and do the hustle with Hossein Attar. She'd Salsa with Darth Vader if that meant she'd get a sub sandwich.

As the lead dancer in life, she communicates with subtle physical signals while we all two-step around her.

"Sorry, sorry, sorry, sorry," Lisa says four hundred times—wearing you out until you are too tired to be mad and have forgotten why she's sorry anyway.

She aims at your soft spot. Your heart melts when she asks "Can I give you a hug?"

We always come back begging for more, even though she toys with our emotions and is the master of the silent treatment.

Never a Heavy Load

Who knew one with so few words could express herself with such wit?

Our brother Mark said it well: "I don't recall a time when she was a burden."

But at a young age, Lisa herself said it best when her oldest brother Derrick had just finished giving her several piggyback rides.

"One more, one more!" she begged

"No, you're too heavy," complained Derrick.

Lisa Jean's response? "I'm not heavy, you're my brudder."

"He ain't heavy, he's my brother..."

How she was so in tune with the Hollies' heartfelt hit, I'll never know.

Laughter, Love, and Life...Oh, and the Textbooks Are Wrong!

*"She was a bright light
and shared that high beam with many."*

—Kathleen Robinson

The textbooks give a lot of dire warnings about Down syndrome. According to Wikipedia: *Those with Down syndrome nearly always have physical and intellectual disabilities. As adults, their mental abilities are typically similar to those of an eight- or nine-year-old. They also typically have poor immune function and generally reach developmental milestones at a later age. They have an increased risk of…congenital heart defects, epilepsy, leukemia, thyroid diseases, and mental disorders, among [other health problems].*

Armed with this distressing prognosis, prenatal testing has increased the number of abortions performed when a child is found to have Down syndrome. About 92 percent of Down syndrome–diagnosed pregnancies in Europe are terminated. The termination rate in the U.S. is around 67 percent.

And this is tragic.

Because what the textbooks don't tell you is about all the love and kindness and laughter that those with Down syndrome bring to the folks around them.

People with Down syndrome have a high beam that shines unconditionally. Their joy is endless. Lisa Jean gave us all purpose and showed us the important life lesson of embracing all people, especially those who are different.

Caring for her was no cakewalk, but Lisa Jean never sold cocaine or stole moonshine from Mom and Dad's liquor cabinet. She never got D's and F's, stole car parts off Eddie Murphy's Ferrari, or slugged her math teacher. She taught me to live in happiness, too, *like the Oompa Loompa Doompety dooooo*. She brought out my inner child, and that child is still having the time of her life. The simplicity of Lisa's light kept mine from going dark.

Lisa's high beam shone in many forms. Never more than the time she charmed her way onstage with Michael Franti and J Bowman, moving her body in not-so-G-rated ways as she partied with her 9,525 new fans. Her side vocation was charming money out of the Big O mechanic's pocket with her warmth and purity; she sweet-talked him with her simplicity.

A Train Runs into a Poison Apple

At the beginning of this book, I compared death to eating a poison apple or being hit by a train. Most times people experience one or the other.

Lisa took a bite of a poison apple in the womb. Put as simply as possible: Down syndrome occurs when an individual has a full or partial extra copy of chromosome 21. This additional genetic material alters the course of development and causes the characteristics associated with Down syndrome.

That includes a decreased life expectancy.

But Lisa took her physical hurdles in stride. When she had to undergo a medical procedure that required she eat and drink only "foods she could see through," she quipped: "How about a donut?"

In her late forties, Lisa was losing her teeth like Stu in the movie *Hangover* and having seizures. Eventually we figured out that these maladies were adult-onset symptoms of Downs. She was combative. She stopped talking. Sometimes her memory was there; often it was not. She was unable to work or attend recreational day programs. She went through a stage where we all had a hard time knowing what was best for her.

And we could measure by the minute her life ticking away. So she moved to New York to be with our brother who was a nurse and could take very good care of her. The move was a blessing, but my center of gravity was upended. My heart lost a beat and the rhythm of life that I knew how to sway with no longer showed me the way.

Our communication was now limited to phone calls. I would call her three to five times a week, but she became more and more difficult to connect with emotionally.

A Concert Cameo

Four months before Lisa's death, I went to New York and took Lisa to a Michael Franti & Spearhead concert. Since her major performance at Red Rocks, Lisa Jean had been to two more of their concerts. The first time, she was again onstage with the band; however, she was unable to find a prominent spot at their next one—an outdoor concert at Colorado's Breckenridge ski area. Due to my recent knee surgery, a three-foot wall of snow in front of the stage, Lisa's limited mobility, and her wheelchair not budging in the icy conditions, we got stalled just past the security fence. Our pal Hossein tried to get her up onstage, but her Oompa-Loompa physique was no match for the elements.

In New York, though, she once again charmed her way backstage and onstage. She waved at Hossein and flashed her ear-to-ear grin, and next thing I knew, we were standing in front of fifteen hundred people beside Michael and J. At the end of that concert, she high-fived the audience at the edge of the stage. I was so sure she was going to crowd surf, I held on to her shirt.

Before that, when we first went backstage, she said maybe five words to the band. But the moment they went out and started playing, she pointed and said clear as day: "I want to give him a hug." (I think she meant Michael, but she could have meant Hossein and/or J because she liked to flirt with them, too.) She came out of her shell and they connected.

And the magic surged both ways. Like the flow of a river—all those watching from the banks rejoiced in the beauty, the power, and the force of nature called Lisa.

Michael's music was the key to unlocking her.

After the concert, we had joyful phone calls again:

"Hi, Lisa," I'd say.

"Are you coming?" she would ask.

"Yes!" I would answer.

Silence.

"Aflac!" I would declare.

Giggle, giggle, she would respond.

"Stinky!" I would say.

She would grin. She was still there.

But slowly over the months that followed, she left again. I would call and she would stare into the phone mutely; then she would wander off to the bathroom.

The Final Encore

Monday, January 23, 2017, was the last time I was in touch with Lisa. I called her in New York from Colorado. We Facetimed so I could see her and remind her of who I was.

But she wouldn't speak to me; she was stone-faced. I tried saying "Aflac" and "Stinky" and "Dr. Pepper" and talking about our dog Twitch. Usually these things got her to laugh.

She wouldn't flinch.

I had Michal Franti & Spearhead playing as I do every morning to get the day started, so I walked the phone over to the speaker and blasted their music at her. Locked away as she was, their song "The Sound of Sunshine" gave her a way to communicate without words. In a final *Dancing with the Stars* encore, she Sliwinska'd her arms over her head and pumped them with jubilation. She twirled and shimmied and shook. She whooped with joy. Her eyes twinkled and her Cheshire-cat grin glowed.

Lisa died of a heart attack on January 28th. I got to see her last dance and her most memorable. She left me with a vision of her smile and buoyancy. She connected the dots by dancing. She filled my heart with love.

Lisa's memory lives on with each song played by Michael Franti & Spearhead. I share her legacy by taking people with special challenges to their concerts. The Do It For The Love Foundation, along with the L. W. Rock Star Memorial Fund I started, helps me give flight to others.

Lisa has been released to spread her rumpled wings with the angels and fly.

Lisa danced through life beating to her own drum. Many say it is I who did so much for her, but words can never express how much more she gave to me. And to so many others. L.J. shared her love, her sense of self, her kindness, and her drollery unconditionally. She was an open book and easy to read if you looked into her soul and were not fearful of the unknown. I loved those who could look into her illumination and not be blinded.

The Power of Lisa

Lisa never pretended to be somebody she was not. This allowed you to also be yourself without second-guessing. She did not work hard at convincing you to like her. She liked herself and that was enough.

She knew what she wanted and she appreciated your help in getting it. She had her wishes: the bathroom, a Diet Dr. Pepper, food, animals, music, and to be onstage with her buddies Michael, J, Hossein, and the rest of the crew.

J made Lisa giggle even when she didn't want to. Michael helped her express herself. Hossein gave her flight by getting her onstage at the concerts. They were the ties that bound us together and brought Lisa out of her shell.

With the encouragement of my daughter, Anna, I called Hossein and J the day Lisa died to tell them the news. They took her loss very hard. They helped me understand how much of a difference Lisa had made to them.

"She brought so much light and love to the band and its support crew," Hossein told me. "Light brings light."

All this time I had thought it was they who had given so much to us, but in reality the giving was mutual.

"It was Lisa who beamed her radiance on those around her and brought tears of joy to their eyes," said J. "She was the magic, and the music brought out the magic."

"Even when Lisa was shut down, you knew she was a powerhouse," said Hossein, "because she did it her way." He added that every time he sees a Dr. Pepper, he thinks of her and it brings a smile to his face.

Lisa's innocence was joyful. Her unconditional love was infectious. Her laugh was contagious. Her wit was a mystery. Her sayings were addictive.

I know L.J. is dancing now with all those we have lost, who took a bite of that apple or encountered a train.

"You're Fired!"

Lisa used to say "You're fired" if she didn't get her way. I guess I got fired from my role as Lisa's dance partner here on Earth.

It felt like losing another of my children. I got in the ring with Lisa and fought her fight as soon as I was able. Come rain or shine, it was easy to stay in her courageous battle.

Love dances in and out of your life in the most unexpected ways. Illumination touches you in dark times when you feel lost. Lisa Jean radiated sunshine into our worlds, keeping us found.

Dancing in the Rain

Some might say having a sister with Down syndrome is like living in a perpetual storm. But Lisa was a soft gentle spring shower in which I felt moved to dance. The daily raindrops were invigorating, energizing, nourishing, awakening, and renewing—and rainbows always peeked out from the dark clouds after difficult downpours. I didn't just live in the rain; I danced and sang and experienced a good ol' hootenanny of sorts.

Lisa's dance partner now is God. She's waltzing from one cloud to another while promising Him a hug if He gets her a Diet Dr. Pepper. Maybe their footsteps on the clouds are why it rains so much love.

28

I'VE NEVER MADE A MISTAKE...

Once I Thought I Did, But I Was Wrong—DEAD Wrong

Everybody's fairy tale has a wicked witch, an evil stepmother, a gang of bandits, and a "slick...sick" Royal Vizier of Agrabah. They disguise themselves as alcoholism, cancer, drug addiction, difficult teenagers, and learning disabilities.

Happy endings are a process. We all have the possibility of everlasting happiness, but we face splats and thumps along the way. It is only if we rejoice in each breath, embracing life and all its dreams, promises, and hopes, imagining each moment as bright, that we can live our fairy tale.

We can draw inspiration from fairy tale characters to reach that happy ending. I emulate Mulan, changing my reality by imagining myself as someone else. Like Elsa from *Frozen*, I use my unique powers to rise above hardships. I aspire to be Pocahontas, embracing nature to find beauty in my world. Like the Genie in *Aladdin*, I find humor in as many moments as possible, even if it cricks my neck.

My husband, who is my real Prince Charming; my children, who have been superstars in each chapter of my life; my father, who was my Bob Hope, silly and selfless; my mother, Carol Burnett: funny and strong; my family; and my friends are my Blue the Bear, Dragon, and Miss Piggy. Lisa Jean was my Olaf: funny, endearing, special, and slowly melting away.

Some figures in my book support me and make me laugh. My own antidotes to the slumps are my quiet obsession with my own creative side, being lucky enough to start my own business, and my humor. They are what make my story one of perseverance and pleasure despite the pain.

When I first climbed into my sparkly blue MINI Coop for the journey of writing this book, my plan was to relate the humorous experiences I have encountered. I aspired to reign as queen of my words, with humor as the zeitgeist of my story. I had no intention of sharing my traumas, because I didn't want them to be the focus. I didn't want my readers to be sideswiped by sorrow.

But my initial reviewers advised me: "You *need* to share your suffering. You can only help people if they know what you've been through and how you've survived. You have to show that you're not just a Pollyanna."

Heeding their advice made me feel like Kermit the Frog; hopping around naked and exposing myself was hard. Sharing my foibles was easy. Talking about my Cabbage Patch Kiddie Breasts was a stretch. But as a friend counseled me, not everything can be funny. And it's true: You must keep moving forward through the positives and negatives to get to the funny parts of life and to meet your Prince Charming.

I've Never Made a Mistake...

Just as I told my husband while jumping naked on the bed after Eliza died: "Please let me grieve." It wasn't that he wasn't letting me grieve; it's that I had to grieve in my way and at my pace. The same goes for my journey I've now shared with you, detailing my highs and lows so that I may help you understand.

I've discovered that my blue MINI Coop plays an important role in my life...aside from being instrumental in the demise of a frog. Along the journey of writing this book, my Coop has carried me through many byways and highways and ups and downs. It's taught me that life can change in an instant, just like it did, for example, on January 28, 2016: I must have legs like that frog because while skiing down a mountain, I blew out my knee, landing me in surgery two weeks later. While a frog wouldn't be skiing, I was bedridden nonetheless; I was not leaping and bounding through the forest for a while. I was forced to see the forest through the trees and put it all in perspective. My knee was repaired, but then a bad decision on my part changed my life yet again, causing another year's recovery from a second pop of my knee ligament.

It could have been worse: I was not like the young man in my community who got hit by a wave and is now paralyzed from the neck down, but who, despite the drastic change in his reality, remains positive and strong. I am not the dear, dear friend who was diagnosed with cancer in August and died in November; I am not my mother-in-law who had a heart attack and died from complications on Valentine's Day.

My life is amazing and I am grateful for it every day. It's thanks to my blue MINI Coop with Fabio, Cabbage Patches, pool boys, Michael Franti, J Bowman, and Hossain, the guy at the ski area who held the door for me the fateful day I blew out my knee, and those closest to me, that I can keep puttering along. I can live my dream to help others with my Bird Herd buddy Yoho (whose name is Kree

I'VE NEVER MADE A MISTAKE...

Indian for awe and wonder), who reminds me to do the same, Razz (short for Razzamatazz), who focuses on the razzle dazzle in the world, and all of my other fine feathered friends. I can try to inspire others and help them through the hard times so that they can keep hopping and bopping along while they get through their slumps and bumps and triumphs in life.

I understand that sometimes GAS will overtake you.

Your MANEtain Toolbox will be locked and you won't have access to the tools to help you find a Laugh of the Day.

Fabio and all his friends will crawl in your bed and together you will wallow in your pity party while singing your favorite songs from the *Sound of Mucus*.

The Crimes Against Your Sanity will rob the heck out of your stamina and strength.

You'll wish LSD could be your drug of choice and that the dang pool boys would let you join in their pot party.

Your old habits will creep into your panties of life and those STDs will remind you that, in fact, you are no longer a virgin to the hardships and challenges of life.

No matter how much you cough Walt Disney's Cough, you'll still feel like the cup is half empty rather than half full.

Life is a Bitch, a Bitch and it would be nice to be Joanie and stay in that damn lamp.

And there will be those days that your lotus will lose its buds and you'll watch your erotica wither.

Remember: When you are in this state of mind, when you do want to eat your young, that "if at first you don't succeed…then sky diving is not for you." Tomorrow is another day and you can get through this. Life is designed in such a way that your next breath is there for you to try again. You have people in your life who can be the "hot iron on the wrinkles of your soul." You've never made a mistake…what you did was learn (as put so insightfully by Danish philosopher Soren Kierkegaard) is that life can only be lived moving forward, but it can only be understood looking back.

So pucker up your lips, coil your legs, and spring forward into your world. Whether an apple is in your reach or a red bull is bearing down on you at a breakneck speed, you can leapfrog through anything.

Remember to smack your lips and communicate, even if you have a frog in your throat.

Don't lollygag in your own swamp.

Don't turn green with envy.

There are snakes out there; avoid them.

It takes time to grow from a polliwog to a frog.

Fill your bog with creative thoughts, love, and laughter.

Don't wallow in your mortifications.

Once you have done something you can't change, rearrange it.

The ripples in your pond are what life brings to you.

"Just keep swimming."

Don't hop to conclusions.

Let death help you live!

Remember: I've never made a mistake…once I thought I did but I was wrong. *DEAD* wrong!

ELIZA, ELIZA

Eliza, Eliza,
Who might you have become?
What paths might you have walked, what adventures dared?
What might you have created? Whom might you have loved?
An empty space where a life should be.
So many might-have-beens—
you seem an unanswered question.

Eliza, Eliza,
What question shall we ask?
Who might have you become? No—too wistful; too indirect.
No, better the question you beckon from beyond our conscious questions:
Who are you?
He who was born the night you were not
once whispered with a loud voice:
"I AM!"
Now silently, so silently,
you, too, shout mutely:
"I AM! I AM! I AM!"
For, brief you have been in time and space,
with little past and no future,
yet blessed with an eternal present,
which present you now give to us,
and give, and give, and give.

Untimely time:
Time to let go, time to be led.
Out of time.
Time for you, time for us—
no longer minutes, to be sure,
but moments, which you and we can share.

Eliza, Eliza,
Lama sabachthani?
Why have you forsaken us, Eliza?
Did you decide never to grow up—
or have you grown up in the twinkling of an eye?
Are we destined never to know you,
or shall we know you with a depth reserved for only a few?
Have you simply left our world,
or have you enlarged it to encompass and be encompassed by your own?

Eliza, Eliza,
You who were, and are, and ever shall be.
We hear your muted cry—
though, in truth, ours is not much louder:
"I AM!"
Life affirmed—yours, ours, God's.
AMEN.

Frank. C. Strasburger
Christmas Day, 1994

ACKNOWLEDGMENTS

In addition to my family, I have an amazing team of professional and personal supporters I wish to thank:

Rob Aukerman, for your talent and artistic eye—I mean, eyes!

Michele Becci, for your unending patience in listening to all my crazy business ideas and for your love of giving to me and to the world.

Tamara Blett, I loved sharing the journey of writing a book with you. I hope your book reaches everyone in the universe!

Margo Burns, for your poem *Dimes,* your helpful critiques, and for you!

Maya Luna Christobel, my spirited writing teacher, for all your encouragement.

Carrie Doman, for the quote "You are a hot iron on the wrinkles of my soul" and for being one of my hot irons.

Suzanne Gabriele, for being my brain.

Rich Levine, for your refreshingly warm and witty attention to detail.

Danny Prinzler, for your poem "The Sound of Home." Thanks for laughing with me.

Jessica Ricalde, my executive assistant. Thank you for keeping me glued!

Kathleen Robinson, for your loving writing guidance and for holding me up in so many ways.

Frank Strasburger, for the *Eliza, Eliza* poem.

Jennifer Thomas, for your fantastic editing skills, for laughing at all the right times, for your true dedication to Allen.

Acknowledgments

My girlfriends, who shine into the dark corners of my world and provide me healing light.

I am grateful to you all. This book couldn't have happened without you!

Finally I'd like to give a shout-out to a few people who have inspired me along my journey:

Brené Brown, for her work on courage and vulnerability.

Sara Franti, for co-founding a foundation that helps those in need.

Rachel Hollis, for empowering women and giving so much of YOU!

Meg Jay, author of *Supernormal: The Untold Story of Adversity and Resilience.*

Angelina Jolie, for sharing your breast cancer story.

Sue Klebold, for your Ted talk "My son was a Columbine shooter. This is my story," raising awareness of needed mental health support.

Monica Lewinsky, for pulling the positive out of a bad situation by speaking out against cyber-bullying in your Ted talk "The Price of Shame."

Trevor Noah, for telling your story and giving others the opportunity to share theirs.

Brian Shannon, author of *Technical Analysis Using Multiple Timeframes,* for using the Adam Smith "invisible hand" to pay it forward.

Jen Sincero, author of the *You Are a Badass* books.

Mother Teresa, for showing the world the impact one person can have even when suffering from STD's (Self-Traumatizing Doubts).

DeOndra Dixon, Kennedy Lewis, Lloyd Lewis, Makenna Plantz, Louis Rotella IV, Anna and John J. Sie, Marcus Sikora, Fran Stephens, and *Michelle Sie Whitten,* for being voices for people with disabilities.

ABOUT THE AUTHOR

Joan Arent is a professional presenter, life coach, painter, sculptor, illustrator, and author. Via her uplifting products and presentations, she educates, empowers, and entertains by sharing "Whimsical Proactive Problem-Solving Skills You Can Play With." Her goal is to motivate people to spread their wings and fly!

Speaking around the world, Joan uses humor to encourage while instilling a key life-changing message: No matter the hurdles, with creative thinking, perseverance, and passion, we can all succeed.

Joan has a Master's Degree in Therapeutic Recreation, Special Education, and Adaptive Physical Education.

With the help of her fun feathered friends, the Bird Herd, Joan also creates products for children. Book titles include *Slumps, Bumps, and Triumphs; Bye, Bye Booger Bug: The Art of Nose Picking;* and *Peek-a-Boo Who?* Based on her longtime experience, she provides coaching to others on how to write, illustrate, and publish their own adult and children's books.

Joan's playful personality and inspiring innovations help individuals of all ages bring joy, laughter, and strength into their lives.

 Join Joan on Facebook!
facebook.com/IveNeverMadeAMistake
facebook.com/groups/FightSTDsWithJoanArent

Discover Playful Ways to Soar in YOUR Life!

A *SOUL*utions Strategist, Joan shares her signature brand of growth mindset with groups and individuals, from multinational corporations to nonprofits and educational institutions, and from international leaders and entrepreneurs to stay-at-home moms.

Tailoring her dynamic, interactive programs to each audience and their unique hurdles, Joan makes the hard changes manageable with humor and encouragement.

Joan is "outrageously funny, incredibly insightful, and irrationally inspiring!"
—Presentation participant

EMPOWERMENT. EDUCATION. ENTERTAINMENT.

Joan is available via video-chat or in person, for:

Keynotes and Presentations

Book Readings and Book Club Visits

Life and Business Coaching

Inspire you and yours by inviting Joan to your ***business, institution, social group,*** or ***school*** to promote positive change!

www.JoanArent.com

LISA JEAN'S
ROCK STAR MEMORIAL FUND

To donate, please visit:

www.lwrockstarmemorial.fund

Or

mail a check made out to:

L. W. Rock Star Memorial Fund

to:

Bank of the West
P.O. Box 339
Conifer, CO 80433

www.ingramcontent.com/pod-product-compliance
Lightning Source LLC
Chambersburg PA
CBHW030438300426
44112CB00009B/1066